SUCCESS WITHOUT COLLEGE

Careers
Cosmetology

Mary L. Dennis

BARRON'S

All inquiries should be addressed to:
Barron's Educational Series, Inc.
250 Wireless Boulevard
Hauppauge, New York 11788
http://www.barronseduc.com

International Standard Book No. 0-7641-1523-5

Library of Congress Catalog Card No. 00-037844

Library of Congress Cataloging-in-Publication Data

Dennis, Mary
 Success without college: careers in cosmetology / Mary Dennis.
  p. cm.
 Includes bibliographical reference and index
 ISBN 0-7641-1523-5 (alk. paper)
  1. Beauty culture—Vocational guidance.   I. Title.
TT958 .D48 2000
646.7'2'023—dc21   00-037844

Printed in the United States of America

9 8 7 6 5 4 3

Table of Contents

TABLE OF CONTENTS

Careers in the Cosmetology Industry

This book was written to help three kinds of job seekers:

• High school students or recent graduates who are unclear about their career direction

• Adults who are interested in entering the cosmetology field

• Cosmetologists who would like to explore other careers closely related to their field

Success Without College: Careers in Cosmetology will help you plan your career in several ways. The book includes a self-test to assess whether or not cosmetology is a career field you should consider.

Also included are descriptions of 11 occupations within the industry that delineate each job's responsibilities, explain licensing requirements, and project earnings and employment demand. You will also find essential information on the education needed for each of the careers profiled, and a list of questions to consider when you evaluate and choose a training program.

In each of the 11 occupation chapters, you'll meet a professional who is now working in the position who will tell you what led him or her to his or her career and what an on-the-job day is like. You'll learn what these professionals like and don't like about their jobs, and you'll read advice on the best way to enter each career.

Like the cosmetology professionals profiled in this book, you can attain success by finding the proper training and by following the job-search strategies outlined in Chapters 14 and 15. You'll learn how to capitalize on job skills you developed at previous seemingly unrelated jobs. You'll find out how to write résumés and cover letters, and how to handle common interview questions. Most important, you'll learn where to look for jobs and how to evaluate the various compensation plans common in the cosmetology field.

With the possible exception of barbering, cosmetology occupations covered in this book are projected to grow at a faster than average rate between now and 2006. Some are growing at a *much* faster rate. Finding qualified staff is one of the biggest challenges reported by salons nationwide. It is definitely a job seeker's market.

All of the cosmetology professionals I spoke with while writing this book showed amazing enthusiasm for their work. Far from fitting the "beauty school bimbo" stereotype, they are immensely honest, intelligent, and hard-working people who really care about others. I hope *Success Without College: Careers in Cosmetology* will help you decide if you want to join this dedicated group who devote their days to helping others look and feel their best.

Mary L. Dennis
Woodslover@aol.com

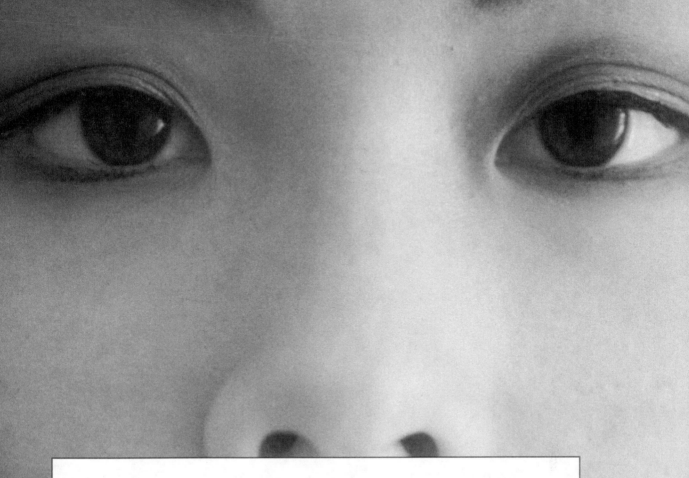

Acknowledgments

I would like to thank the following individuals, organizations, and publications, without whose help this book would not have been possible: The American Electrology Association; the American Massage Therapy Association; the Cosmetology Advancement Foundation; Intercoiffure America; Mary Bird at the National Accrediting Commission of Cosmetology Arts and Sciences; Jose Artigas at the International Academy of Hair Design; Denise Rucci at the Barber and Beauty Supply Institute; John Payne at Hair International; Jami Derr, Karin Cadle, Kasey Walker, Debbie Vega, Kathy Kirkland at *Nailpro Magazine*; Theresa Lewis at OPI; *Nails Magazine*; Dee Manieri, Donna Marie Amadori-Tucker, Dave Pitruzzello at Salon Elite; Sheryl Baba at Paparazzi Studio; Crystal Wright at *1st Hold Magazine*; Susan Church at the International Institute of Permanent Cosmetics; the Society of Permanent Cosmetic Professionals; the International Guild of Professional Electrologists; Tracey Francis, Sharon Kizziah-Holmes, Bill Laswell, Jacob Moore, Zeb Thomas, Amy Craddock, Ed Pacyna, Lori Dutruel, Associated Bodywork and Massage Professionals; Mary Scott-Rom at Kirtland Community College; and Dan Leaser, Rose Charney, and Jackie McGinnis at the Pennsylvania Academy of Cosmetology Arts and Sciences.

I am also indebted to Grace Freedson and Mark Miele of Barron's Educational Series and to my husband, Wayne Thomas, who encouraged and supported me every step of the way.

CHAPTER ONE

Your Future in Cosmetology

Cosmetologists care for people's hair, skin, and nails. They are in the business of making people look good and feel good about themselves. Watch television for an hour, or flip through an issue of *Allure* or *Gentlemen's Quarterly*, and it is easy to see how important it is to women and men of all ages to look and feel their best. Cosmetology is a growing field with a positive job outlook. The demand for qualified cosmetologists far outweighs the number available to fill job slots.

COSMETOLOGY: A FEEL-GOOD BUSINESS

Only 100 years ago, professional hairstyling, manicures, and facials were possible only for the wealthy. Now they are affordable for almost everyone. More women work outside the home than ever before, and it is important to them to appear well groomed and stylish. The same women, stressed out from the demands of full-time jobs and families, have increased the demand for day spas, where they enjoy relaxing massages, facials, and special services. In increasing numbers, men are spending time and money on personal care services as well. Twenty-five percent of those visiting spas in 1999 were men, and men who wouldn't have gone near a "beauty shop" a few decades ago are now regular customers.

The development of many new products promising to reverse or halt aging means an increased demand for facials, peels, and other skin procedures. Hair colorists revitalize graying hair, electrologists remove unwanted hair, and makeup artists help clients retain their youthful looks. The aging of the "Baby Boomers" translates into more business.

Salons are everywhere. Whether you live in a small town, big city, or suburb, there is probably a salon within a few miles of your home. There are chain salons offering no-appointment-needed services, as well as small independent salons. You can find salons in department stores, shopping malls, hotels, hospitals, and retirement communities.

Some cosmetologists offer in-home services to elderly clients and others who find it difficult to travel to the salon. Cosmetologists in the television, theater, and film industry spend their time backstage or in the wings, always ready to touch up a celebrity's makeup or hairstyle. Others work in the fashion industry, styling hair and making up models for photo shoots or live fashion shows. You can even find cosmetologists working in funeral homes.

Cosmetologists take pride in their ability to transform the ordinary into the extraordinary and to watch their clients' moods and attitudes change too. The delight and appreciation of a satisfied client is one of the most rewarding aspects of the job.

JOB MARKET: LOOKIN' GOOD

Cosmetology is one of the fastest-growing fields in the nation. According to a recent job demand survey conducted for the National Accrediting Commission of Cosmetology Arts and Sciences, salon owners indicated that they planned to fill 500,000 positions in the first six months of 1999. In fact, about 75 percent of the salon owners who looked for new employees in the previous year had trouble finding qualified people. It is definitely a job seeker's market.

The *Occupational Outlook Handbook*, published by the U.S. Department of Labor, put the national average salary for a hair stylist in 1997 at $17,350, but most industry leaders feel that figure is very misleading because 40 percent of those employed in the field work part time and because tips comprise so much of a cosmetologist's earnings. (Tips are often not accurately reported to the government.) Another reason it is difficult to give an accurate earnings figure is that there are several different ways cosmetologists are compensated.

In the 1999 job demand survey mentioned, NACCAS found the average hourly wage for cosmetologists to be about $18.50 per hour, including tips. A *National Business Employment Weekly* survey (*Jobs Rated Almanac, 3rd Edition*, written by Les Krantz and published by John Wiley and Sons) found $21,000 to be the average salary for a beginner, with mid-level earnings at $27,000 and top earnings at $42,000. The Economic Research Institute predicts that by the year 2015, the mean salary for a cosmetologist will be $44,729.

How much can you expect to make? The answer is, it's really up to you. Almost everyone in the industry agrees that low starting wages are the norm. Beginning cosmetologists have no established clientele (loyal customers who return again and again). If you can build a client base and then continually add new clients and learn new techniques, the chances are good that you will succeed and that your earnings will steadily increase. A lot will also depend on where you live and in what kind of salons you work.

TYPICAL CAREER PATHS

Beginning cosmetologists don't usually start out as platform artists or stylists on cruise ships. Many cosmetologists start out in a chain salon that offers quick haircuts and styles on a walk-in basis. In many communities, these chain salons regularly hire graduates of local beauty schools, expecting the new hires to leave after they gain some experience and build a customer base.

Many cosmetologists view their first jobs as stepping-stones to greater things. As they develop their own creative style techniques—and a list of satisfied clientele—they are in a better position to move to upscale salons or to begin looking at some of the more glamorous opportunities within the profession.

Mary Bird, of the National Accrediting Commission of Cosmetology Arts and Sciences, says, "If a person is a go-getter, he or she can go anywhere in the cosmetology field." She also points out that a cosmetology license can be the means to additional education as well. Flexible scheduling on the job means that cosmetologists can easily work while attending college. A degree in business, or even a single basic accounting course, can be of great value to someone opening his or her own salon. Psychology and salesmanship classes are useful in every aspect of the industry.

> ### Career Opportunities
> Some career opportunities available in the cosmetology industry include:
>
> - Professional Stylist
> - Nail Technician
> - Skin Esthetician
> - Permanent Makeup Technician
> - Electrologist
> - Makeup Artist
> - Massage Therapist
> - Cosmetology School Instructor, Administrator, or Owner
> - Manufacturer's Representative/Educator
>
> You'll learn more about these and other fields in the following chapters.

IS COSMETOLOGY FOR YOU?

Choosing a career is one of the most important decisions you will ever make. You can choose a job you'll like so well you'll be one of those lucky people who say, "I can't believe I'm getting paid for this!" Or, you can make the wrong decision and dread going in to work every day. If you are trying to decide if you want to pursue a career in cosmetology, there are several things you can do.

1. Try to get a part-time job at a salon, even if all you do is sweep up hair. Then try to put yourself in the place of the stylist, nail technician, or esthetician. Eavesdrop. Would you like to do what they are doing?

2. Ask at your own salon if you can spend a few Saturdays just observing. When an employee has some free time, ask him or her about job demands and satisfactions. Get some opinions on schools in your area. Which one has the best reputation? What courses could you take now, if you are still in high school, that would prepare you for the classes you will take in cosmetology school?

3. If you are still in high school, ask your guidance director if you can take some career assessment tests. Some examples are the Strong Interest Inventory, the California Occupational Preference System (COPS), the Career Ability Placement Survey (CAPS), and the Myers-Briggs Type Indicator. Your counselor can help you interpret the results to see if you have the mental aptitude and personality traits to find satisfaction and success in cosmetology. If you are no longer in high school, check with the counseling department of your local community college. The counselors there may administer these or similar tests free of charge or for a small fee.

The short test on the following pages will help you zero in on the basic skills and traits you need in order to succeed as a cosmetologist. Search within yourself for an honest answer to each question.

By answering the questions on the "Cosmetology Self-Test" honestly you will be better able to determine whether a career as a professional stylist, nail technician, makeup artist, or one of the many other professions available today in the cosmetology field is right for you.

COSMETOLOGY SELF-TEST

	Yes	No

1. Are you in good health? Do you have the energy to work on your feet all day and use your arms and hands almost constantly? Will you be bothered by exposure to hair dyes, waving solutions, and other chemicals?

2. Are you able to get along well with others in a work environment, even when some of them are irritable or irritating?

3. Do you have a genuine desire to make other people look and feel better about how they look?

4. Can you learn from criticism and complaints rather than getting angry or dissolving into tears?

5. If a client told you a bit of intriguing information in confidence, could you keep his or her secret?

6. Can you keep smiling even when you are being pushed to your limits to accomplish a lot in a specified length of time?

7. Are you good at planning your daily schedule so that no time is wasted?

8. Will you be willing to spend the time and money necessary to keep up with new trends and methods? (This means reading beauty magazines, attending trade shows, and learning new techniques in workshops and classes.)

9. Will you have no problem working evenings and weekends even if it means missing out on activities with friends?

10. Do you spend a lot of time looking at people's hair, nails, and makeup and thinking how they could be improved? Do you read every word of the hair and makeup articles in magazines?

	Yes	No

11. Are you willing to put in the hours of study in cosmetology school to (a) get all of the credits you need, and (b) study for and pass the state boards?   _____   _____

12. Will you be able to accept and carry out instructions from a customer even if you feel the end results will be unsatisfactory?   _____   _____

If you answered "Yes" to most of the questions in the self-test, the cosmetology field may well be for you. If you have a few "No" answers, think about how willing you are to change.

For example, you can learn to manage stress and improve your physical endurance, but if you recoil at the idea of someone criticizing your work, or if you insist on having weekends off, you may need to rethink your career direction.

There is much more to cosmetology than just cutting and styling hair. Cosmetologists are also trained to give manicures and pedicures; scalp, hair, and facial treatments; and to color hair. They also provide makeup advice and instruction.

In addition to completing cosmetology school (or, in some states, apprenticing with a licensed cosmetologist), they need to possess certain attributes: the stamina to stand on their feet all day, the ability to interact pleasantly with clients who may sometimes be irritable, an aptitude for getting along with other employees who are in the same work area all day, and excellent time-management skills.

State, national, and international conventions and events keep cosmetologists up to date on the newest products and trends in the business. Attendees can take classes in hair, makeup, esthetics, and nails and listen to motivational speakers and business experts. Contacts made at such events can be valuable later on.

Many people are surprised to find that cosmetology is a science as well as a creative art. Cosmetology students must learn about bacteriology, sanitation, hair analysis, chemistry, and anatomy and physiology. In most states, they must pass a written examination as well as a hands-on practical exam in order to be licensed.

If you have a natural appreciation of beauty, enjoy interacting with new people every day, and find satisfaction in creating with your own hands, cosmetology may be a field you want to investigate further.

RESOURCES

Some books about career choices:

Bolles, Richard Nelson and Dick Bolles. *What Color Is Your Parachute? 2000* Berkely, CA: Ten Speed Press, 1999.

Edwards, Paul and Sarah. *Finding Your Perfect Work*. Los Angeles, CA: J.P. Tarcher, Inc., 1996.

Janda, Louis. *Career Tests: 25 Revealing Self-Tests to Help You Find and Succeed at the Perfect Career*. Holbrook, MA: Adams Media Corp., 1999.

Otterbourg, Robert. *It's Never Too Late: 150 Men and Women Who Changed Their Careers*. Hauppauge, NY: Barron's Educational Series, Inc., 1993.

FOR MORE INFORMATION, CONTACT:

National Cosmetology Association
401 North Michigan Avenue
Chicago, IL 60611-4255
Phone: (312) 644-6610
Web site: *http://www.nca-now.com*

A FEW KEY POINTS TO REMEMBER

- Cosmetologists help people look good and feel good about themselves.
- Cosmetology is a growing field with a very positive job outlook.
- There are varied career paths and diverse opportunities available in the cosmetology industry.
- Take the "Cosmetology Self-Test" on pages 6–7. Your answers will help determine whether a career in cosmetology is right for you.
- You should consider your choice carefully before deciding to become a cosmetologist.
- If you are motivated, there is no limit to how far you can go in the cosmetology field.

CHAPTER TWO

Preparing for a Career in Cosmetology

I n every state, cosmetologists must pass a state board examination in order to become licensed. Until you have your license, you cannot legally practice cosmetology. Training courses at high schools, vocational schools, beauty schools, and community colleges teach you what you need to know in order to pass the board exam for your particular state. Requirements vary from state to state, but most require between 1,200 and 1,600 classroom hours of study. There is a minimum age of 16 or 17, and entrants are usually required to have completed at least the ninth grade. Some programs require a high school diploma or GED. In a few states, you may work as an apprentice cosmetologist for a specific number of hours and then take your licensing exam.

TYPES OF PROGRAMS

HIGH SCHOOL

Many high schools offer programs where a student may spend part of the day studying cosmetology and another part completing requirements for a high school diploma. Students take a three-year or four-year program in cosmetology, beginning in either ninth or tenth grade. Arrangements with area beauty colleges allow students to take additional hours, if needed, after graduation.

The Vocational Industrial Clubs of America stresses the acquisition of skills needed by anyone entering the business world directly from high school. VICA members learn such skills as how to write a good résumé and cover letter and how to dress for a job interview. You can find out if there is a school in your area offering a VICA program by calling (703) 777-8810.

Two advantages of taking classes during high school are that you pay no tuition and you are getting a head start on a career. One disadvantage of some high school programs is that there is no training salon where students can get hands-on experience. This part of the training still has to be completed in a private beauty school, vocational school, or community college before the student can take the state licensing exam.

VOCATIONAL-TECHNICAL SCHOOLS

Vocational-technical schools offer comprehensive training programs that prepare students to pass the state licensing exams. Vo-tech schools offer classes to high school students in lieu of their regular high school programs, and also admit adults in the community who are training for a new career. Students learn about hair, scalp, and skin care; coloring, cutting, and waving hair; decontamination and infection control; barbering and salon management; nail technology and terminology; professional ethics; personal appearance; and other basic cosmetology topics. After completing a certain number of class hours, they are eligible to work in the school salon.

COMMUNITY COLLEGES

Community colleges are another training option. Some offer one-year certificate programs in cosmetology that are similar to those offered by private beauty schools. McLennan Community College in Waco, Texas, offers two choices for those interested in a cosmetology license. A two-year half-day program is offered to students who are still in high school, while a one-year certificate program is available for high school or GED graduates.

At Sandhills Community College in Pinehurst, North Carolina, students who successfully complete the two-year cosmetology program are awarded an Associate in Applied Science Degree. The curriculum includes 66 credit hours of coursework in English, math, art, psychology, basic computer literacy, and business, as well cosmetology courses and hands-on salon work. Are you wondering, "Why those extra classes?" English and psychology will help you improve communication with customers and other employees. A good understanding of mathematical measurement and geometry helps with detailed precision cuts. Art and design classes help you hone your artistic skills, which will apply directly to your work. You can attend community college full time or part time, which is convenient if you need to work while you're taking your cosmetology training. Sandhills also offers a cosmetology program leading to a diploma (40 credit hours), and a certificate course, with no general education courses required (44 credit hours).

PRIVATE BEAUTY SCHOOLS

Another path to a cosmetology career is completion of a course at a private beauty school. Schools go by various names: beauty academy, school of hair design, beauty culture school, and so on. At the International Academy of Hair Design (IAHD) in South Daytona, Florida, the school's stated goal is to establish a thorough and complete knowledge of cosmetology and good professional habits. Students are encouraged to develop an attractive appearance and a pleasant personality. The program consists of the study of theory, practice, demonstrations, lectures, and examinations.

IAHD has a unique "relationship-building" component in which students learn to build their client bases as well as their contacts within the industry. The objective of the Cosmetology Program, as at all beauty schools, is to train students in the competencies needed to pass the state board of cosmetology examination, and to provide students with the foundations that will lead them to successful careers in the cosmetology field. Like community colleges, private schools offer flexible scheduling. Students may be full-time day students, half-time day, or half-time night.

How Many Graduate?

The National Cosmetology Association estimates that about 65 percent of students who enter private beauty school graduate, 40 to 50 percent of those in vocational-technical or community college programs graduate, and 20 percent of high school students enrolled in the cosmetology curriculum actually complete it.

The effectiveness of training available through apprenticeships depends on several factors:

1. the requirements the particular state cosmetology board places on the supervisor of the apprenticeship program
2. the teaching skills of the supervising cosmetologists
3. the time available for instruction, discussion, and hands-on training
4. the willingness of salon staff to help the apprentice learn

An apprentice we observed at a busy salon spent his time doing three things: shampooing clients' hair, performing various cleaning tasks, and going to the back room to get supplies needed by the staff. "I don't know how we ever got along without him," said one of the stylists, "but I don't think he's had a chance to learn much—we're always so busy."

The lesson here is that if you opt for apprenticeship training, ask your state board about its guidelines and how they are enforced. Make sure that you and your supervisor have the same conceptions about what you will be doing, and that you both have the same goal: your successful completion of the licensing exam.

FINDING A SCHOOL

- If you have access to the Internet, your search for the beauty schools in your area can be a simple process. At *http://www.beautyschool.com*, you will find state listings (also Canada and Puerto Rico) of licenses available, the number of hours required, the minimum requirements for entrance, and the address of each state's board of cosmetology or other licensing department. Also included is a list of schools with addresses and telephone numbers. Some have web sites you can access for more information, including descriptions of courses and fees. In many cases, you can contact them on-line for additional information.

- If you do not have access to the Internet, you can begin by finding the address of your state's cosmetology board in Appendix A at the end of this book. Write or call, and ask for information about the licenses offered in your state and the requirements for licensing. The agency may also be able to send you a list of accredited schools.

- If you are still in high school, talk to your guidance counselor to find out if your public school system offers a comprehensive high school or vocational-technical cosmetology program. He or she will be able to tell you all about the program and how to enter it.

- Check with the counseling department of your local community college as well. If the college offers a cosmetology program, the counselor can tell you about the various options offered, send you a catalog, and tell you what you need to do to apply.

It is important to evaluate each school you are considering. To begin with, if you are considering several private beauty schools, contact the National Accrediting Commission of Cosmetology Arts and Sciences to find out if a school is accredited. This means they have met certain established national standards of performance. NACCAS is officially recognized by the U.S. Department of Education as an accrediting agency for cosmetology schools, that is, NACCAS makes sure the schools it lists have met the standards. You can contact them by phone, in writing, or by visiting their web site. Contact information is at the end of this chapter.

Mary Bird, Director of the Government Relations and Legal Department at NACCAS, recommends that you also consider the following before selecting any school:

1. Is the school licensed by the state board of cosmetology?

2. What is the graduation rate for students who enroll in this school program?

3. At what rate do graduates pass the state licensing examination?

4. How long is the program? Will you be able to attend regularly for the required weeks and months? Would you be better off taking a shorter program so you can work in the field while completing a longer program?

5. Are you prepared to meet the physical, artistic, business, and other demands of working in the cosmetology field?

TUITION CONCERNS

Let us suppose you've narrowed your school choice down to one. You've been accepted to the program. Now—how do you pay for it? Various types of financial aid are available for qualified cosmetology students. The federal government offers the Pell Grant, Federal Supplemental Education Opportunity Grant, and Stafford and Perkins loans. Counselors at any cosmetology school, public or private, can help you with the forms you need to submit to apply for financial aid. The NACCAS web site is also a great place to explore the various types of financial aid available.

Another source of financial aid is the Access to Cosmetology Education grants program (ACE), a collaborative effort between the Beauty and Barber Supply Institute, the Cosmetology Advancement Foundation, and the American Association of Cosmetology Schools. ACE scholarships are given in amounts up to $1,000. For more information, access their web site at: *http://www.ace-grant.org* or call their toll-free number, 888-411-GRANT.

You can also consider working while attending school part time. Try to find something related to the cosmetology field. You might work at a cosmetics counter in a department store, drugstore, or beauty supply store, or as a receptionist at a salon.

FOR MORE INFORMATION, CONTACT:

National Accrediting Commission of Cosmetology Arts and Sciences
901 North Stuart Street, Suite 900
Arlington, VA 22203-1816
Phone: (703) 527-7600
Web site: *http://www.naccas.com*

Cosmetology Advancement Foundation
1 Blachley Road
Stamford, CT 06922
Phone: (203) 357-5888
Web site: *http://www.cosmetology.org*

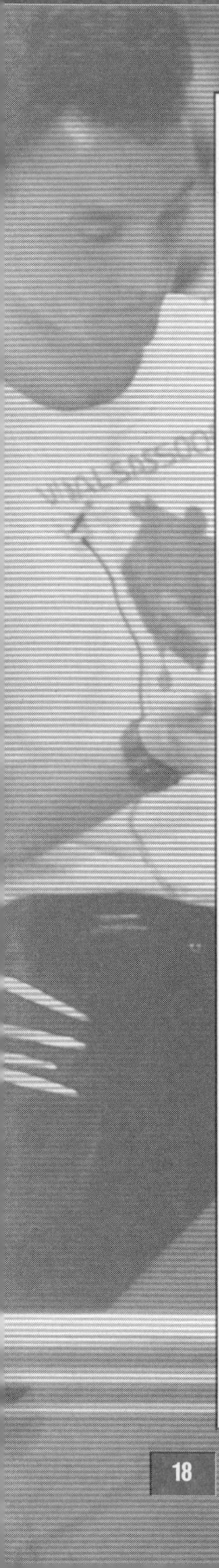

American Association of Cosmetology Schools
11811 N. Tatum Boulevard, Suite 1085
Phoenix, AZ 85028-1625
Phone: (800) 831-1086
Web site: *http://www.beautyschools.org*

Beauty and Barber Supply Institute
11811 N. Tatum Boulevard, Suite 1085
Phoenix, AZ 85028-1625
Phone: (800) 468-2274
Web site: *http://www.bbsi.org*

National Cosmetology Association
401 N. Michigan Avenue
Chicago, IL 60611-4255
Phone: (312) 644-6610
Web site: *http://www.NCA-now.com*

RESOURCES

American Salon Magazine
270 Madison Avenue
New York, NY 10016

Modern Salon Magazine
P.O. Box 1414
Lincolnshire, IL 60069

Salon News Magazine
P.O. Box 5035
Bentwood, TN 37024-9809

A FEW KEY POINTS TO REMEMBER

• In every state, cosmetologists must pass a state board examination in order to be licensed.

• There are four main places where cosmetology classes are offered: high schools, vocational-technical schools, community colleges, and private beauty schools.

• The Internet is a great place to research your state's licensing requirements and available programs.

• If the school of your choice is a private one, make sure it is accredited by NACCAS.

• Financial aid is available for vocational-technical, community college, and private school programs.

CHAPTER THREE

Hairstylist

At the age of five, Kasey Walker knew what she wanted to be when she grew up—a hairstylist. She began practicing right then on her dolls. "After I had cut them all bald, I started on the neighborhood kids," she laughs.

THE RIGHT STUFF

Hairstylists need a sense of symmetry and an artistic flair. They must be able to use their hands and fingers with skill. Good stylists know about hair textures and the way hair grows and falls. They know how to correct hair that is in poor condition. These basic skills are part of the training stylists receive in cosmetology school.

John Payne, president of Hair International, notes that the ability to handle job stress, good social skills, and honesty are also needed by hairstylists. When the pressure is on and the salon is busy, "people skills" are a must. "The worst thing is feeling rushed," says Kathy, a Kansas stylist. "If our appointments are booked too close, or we are trying to fit in walk-ins, we can all get a little edgy. One of the best things you can have at a time like that is a good sense of humor."

Customers may be any age, race, or nationality. They may be shy or friendly, easygoing or demanding. Stylists must be genuinely interested in all kinds of people and deal tactfully with any problems that arise. "I love it when people bring me a picture of what they want," says Kasey Walker. "It gives me a good idea of where we're going and how I can please that customer. Sometimes, though, people can't understand why I can't style their hair to look exactly like the picture. Maybe the model has thick hair, for example, and my client's is baby fine. There is just no way it's going to look like the picture, no matter how skilled the stylist is. So I have to explain that, and maybe suggest how we could adapt that style to suit her hair."

"You have to be a caretaker type and really enjoy listening," says Debbie Vega, a stylist at a J.C. Penney Salon. "We once attended a workshop given by a therapist. He told us it takes him months to get his clients to tell him things they tell us during their first cut. I think it's because we're touching them, and that establishes trust. If you've got someone's trust, that's worth a lot, and you have to be the kind of person who values it."

WHAT HAIRSTYLISTS DO

Hairstylists cut, trim, shape, and style hair. They may also shampoo, color, highlight, wave, and straighten hair. They do weaves, color correction, elaborate braids, and other special styles. Hairstylists use scissors, razors, brushes, curlers, curling irons, dryers, and many types of shampoos, conditioners, styling aids, and chemicals to produce the desired effects.

When they are not working directly with hair, stylists are often involved in learning more about the latest styling techniques. Seminars and workshops, given by education representatives from various beauty supply companies, are fun and informative. Everyone looks forward to "hair shows," where they can see demonstrations of new techniques and check out new products. Motivational speakers and tax experts are helpful, too.

Many beginning stylists work for one of the chains, where they receive a guaranteed wage plus commission on their services and any retail sales they make. Working for a chain is a good way to build clientele when you're first starting out. The chains tend to be located in high-traffic areas like malls, so there are plenty of walk-ins who may later request a particular stylist.

"I started out at a chain," explains Kasey. "Then it got so when I'd come in, I'd have my appointment book full of people who had requested me. I knew I was on my way."

Debbie's job at the J.C. Penney salon near her home is ideal for several reasons. Working for such a large company means she has access to benefits that are often hard to find in the cosmetology business. Some of these include a 401(k) plan, paid holidays, vacations, and sick days, medical and dental insurance, and life insurance.

"For me, it's the best of both worlds," says Debbie. "Since my husband is in business for himself, and individual health insurance is ridiculously expensive, I'm thankful I can cover both of us and all three kids through my work. It's a super place to work for lots of other reasons, too. There is lots of room for advancement within the company. When I was in school, I got so tired of my friends teasing me with that song, 'Beauty School Dropout,' from *Grease*. They aren't laughing now, though!"

Everyone in a chain salon benefits from company-provided advertising on national and local levels. Supplies and tools, except styling scissors, are usually provided. Another advantage is that the stylist has a foot in the door for higher positions such as management or education.

The other earnings options for hairstylists are working on straight commission or renting a chair. In the first arrangement, the stylist and salon owner agree on a percentage each will receive from each service and retail sale. Typically, this runs between 50 and 70 percent to the stylist and the remainder to the salon. Arrangements are also made regarding who pays for supplies. In some salons, where all the stylists are on commission, each one pays a part of the salary of the receptionist, who schedules appointments for everyone.

Chair Rental

"Chair rental" means that the stylist rents space in the salon. Aside from monthly rent, the stylist keeps all the money taken in. While this may sound like the best deal going, there are additional expenses that must be considered such as liability insurance, advertising, and additional record keeping. Neither straight commission or chair rental are workable for beginning stylists, since they have no established clientele; chair rental is illegal in some states. (Your cosmetology board can tell you if state law prohibits chair rental.) A fourth option is to own your own salon.

WHAT THE JOB IS *REALLY* LIKE

Because salons are regulated by the health department, most are clean and comfortable places to work, although stylists spend a great deal of time on their feet. The stylist is assigned a work area where he or she keeps supplies. There may be a sink for shampoos at his or her station or another area where the stylist or a shampooer washes clients' hair.

In a typical day, Kasey Walker shampoos, cuts, styles, straightens, conditions, highlights, perms, and colors hair. She also gives clients advice on hair care and, like most stylists, listens to their stories about their lives. Most days are busy, but on the weekends and during the holidays, they can get hectic. Although the salon where Kasey works is a specialty full-service hair, nail, and facial salon, she works only in the hair department.

While only 60 percent of salon employees work full time, according to a national survey conducted by the National Accrediting Commission of Cosmetology Arts and Sciences in January, 1999, the hours that even the part timers work tend to be evening and weekend hours, when they are needed the most. It is not uncommon for full-time stylists to put in 45 to 50 hours in a busy week. "I love my profession" says Dave Pitruzzello, a Connecticut salon owner and stylist, "but when I put in a lot of hours I sure do miss my kids."

A Person
Who's Done It

MEET KASEY WALKER

VITAL STATISTICS

Kasey, 29, is from San Antonio, Texas. After high school graduation, Kasey completed a cosmetology course at San Antonio Beauty College. Kasey calls the day she received her cosmetology license "the happiest day of my life."

By the time I was in high school, I had learned enough on my own to do some pretty decent cuts on my friends and family. I thought it was important to complete high school, so I did, but I could hardly wait to graduate, and I started beauty school right away. The science classes there were tough, but I knew I had to pass them to get where I wanted to go, so I worked hard.

For a cosmetology license in Texas, the total number of classroom hours required is 1,500. I learned regulations governing the profession, discovered the purpose and composition of chemicals used in hair, nail, and skin care, and learned about health and safety, the use of electrical devices, sanitation, anatomy, scalp treatments, skin care, manicures and pedicures, and hair removal.

Instructors also spent a lot of time preparing us for the state boards. Even though I planned to work only with hair, I had to complete coursework for nail and skin care in order to obtain my cosmetology license.

I was hired almost immediately by a franchise salon and began working full time. When my daily schedule got to the point where it was filled mostly with clients who had found me when they came in as "walk-ins" and then returned to request me specifically, I decided to move on to a different type of work environment.

At the next salon, I worked on straight commission. I concentrated harder on building a following and also began working in the *Look Good...Feel Better* Cancer Patient Program, sponsored by the National Cosmetology Association. This program helps cancer patients deal with the appearance-related side effects of chemotherapy and radiation treatments.

I was especially fond of one of my elderly clients who was ill and home-bound. Well, the woman's grandson came to visit from Florida. I met him while I was on a house call to do his grandmother's hair. It was instant love, and in a few months I was on my way to Fort Myers, Florida, to join Dusty.

Everyone can't just pick up and leave and find a job doing what they love, but that's one advantage of styling hair. I was able to obtain a cosmetology license in Florida through reciprocity with Texas, since Florida requires fewer hours for licensure (1,200). I got a job right away.

Shortly after I joined Scott's Salon Royale in Fort Myers, I participated in a southwest Florida event called Women's Expo. We gave haircuts for $10. The proceeds went to breast cancer research. It's an annual event, and hundreds of salons all over the country participate, so it's kind of exciting to feel part of it all.

In addition to contributing to a good cause, I met many new clients this way who later made appointments with me at the salon. Then some of those people referred friends and family members, and that is how you build a business.

My goal is to one day be a nationally recognized stylist. In the meantime, I look forward to going to work every day and I am still thrilled to have the job I have always wanted.

GETTING IN AND MOVING UP

Before you can get in, you must obtain your license according to the laws of your state, but Dave Pitruzzello says salons are the best place to really *learn*. He advises beginning stylists to "Find a positive boss and go do it!" Getting hired may well include your doing a sample cut as part of your "interview," so bring your favorite scissors, and be prepared.

Getting established during the first few years is one of the biggest challenges of the job. It takes two to three years to "build a book." "My first year, I made just what they told me to expect, $12,000. But I hung in there. Now, in my third year, I make more than double that," explains Debbie Vega. "Sometimes I just can't believe how well things have turned out. Just a few years ago I was a struggling single mom. This year, I attended hair shows in New York and Paris!"

Hairstyling is an evolving business, and stylists have to evolve with it. They learn by watching others in their salons and at trade shows, by taking workshops and seminars, and by watching videos and reading magazines. John Payne, president of Hair International, advises new hairstylists to get as much education as they can to make them more marketable.

A 16-hour course in hair braiding, for example, can bring new clients; a new method for doing highlights can save time. With an established clientele, earnings can increase with a move to a salon where prices are higher, increasing commissions and tips accordingly.

While 87 percent of stylists work in salons, there are other possibilities. Television and movie studios employ hairstylists, as do fashion designers and modeling agencies. Stylists work on cruise ships, at spas and hotels, and as representatives for supply companies. With advanced training, stylists can work as instructors in cosmetology schools or even serve on their state cosmetology boards.

And there is always the dream of becoming an internationally famous stylist with your own line of products, tools, and salons. Why not?

EMPLOYMENT FORECAST

There is general agreement that the first few years as a hairstylist are difficult, but finding a job is not. The industry welcomes new beauty school graduates and people who are reentering the field after some time off. According to a NACCAS 1999 Job Demand Survey, of 180,000 positions left vacant by those leaving the profession in 1998, 100,000 were filled by people with less than one year of experience.

EARNINGS

There is considerable controversy over an average earnings figure for hairstylists. Industry leaders are appalled at the Bureau of Labor's 1997 estimate of $8.34 an hour. They point out that almost half of stylists work part time, driving down the average earnings figure. According to the NACCAS survey mentioned above, $18.50 an hour is closer to a realistic figure for a stylist with an established clientele. Earnings are very much a function of the location and prices of the salon. A part time stylist at the chain salon, where a cut costs $10, is going to make a lot less than the full-time stylist at the best salon in town, where the cuts begin at $30.

PROFESSIONAL CONNECTIONS

Cosmetology Advancement Foundation
208 E. 51st Street
New York, NY 10022
Phone: (212) 388-2771

National Cosmetology Association
401 N. Michigan Avenue
Chicago, IL 60611
Phone: (312) 644-6610
Web site: *http://NCA-now.com*

RESOURCES

American Salon
270 Madison Avenue
New York, NY 10016

Modern Salon
P.O. Box 1414
Lincolnshire, IL 60069

Snip Magazine
(on-line e-zine): *http://www.snipmagazine.com*

A FEW KEY POINTS TO REMEMBER

- Hairstylists need a sense of symmetry, artistic flair, and the ability to work well with their hands.
- Stylists are in close personal contact all day with fellow employees and with customers.
- In order to be successful, hairstylists must stay on top of the latest trends and techniques by participating in continuing education classes.
- There are several ways to earn money as a stylist: hourly wage plus commission, straight commission, or chair rental.
- Getting established during the first few years is one of the biggest challenges stylists face.

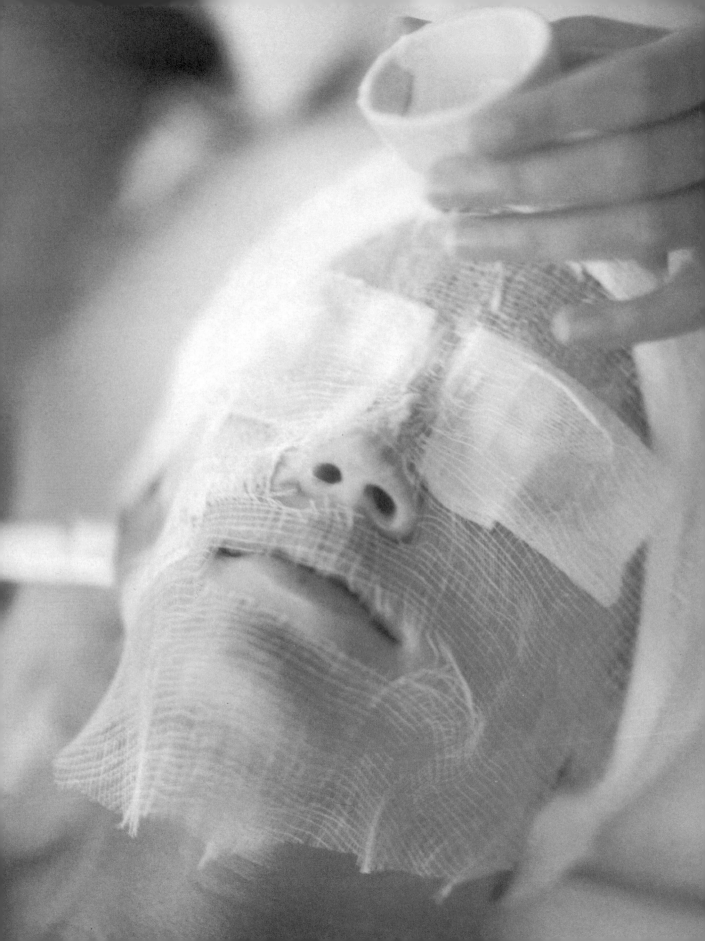

CHAPTER FOUR

Esthetician

S ome people are fortunate enough to have smooth and flawless complexions, but most people's skin is less than perfect. Estheticians—also called aestheticians, facialists, skin care specialists, and cosmeticians—specialize in the care of the skin, particularly that of the face.

THE RIGHT STUFF

Jami Derr, an esthetician in Bethlehem, Pennsylvania, loves the opportunity she has to help clients feel better about themselves. "Especially teenagers. They need to hear what wonderful people they are!" Jami adds, "You have to like your job or it will definitely show through to your client. The focus should be on doing the best you can for your clients, and the financial rewards will automatically follow."

Sheryl Baba, a licensed esthetician in Cape Cod, enjoys her profession so much that she volunteers at her local beauty/esthetic school. She emphasizes goal setting and the art of marketing oneself. "Our services are perceived as a luxury and have a much higher price, so they are more challenging to book than many other salon services," notes Sheryl. "Those in our profession must strive for and maintain the highest standards."

WHAT ESTHETICIANS DO

Basic skin care is taught at cosmetology school. You will learn analysis, physiology, and function of skin. You will also study diseases and disorders because it is important to be able to recognize conditions that require a dermatologist's care.

When Karin Cadle, 28, became interested in the esthetics field, everyone she asked told her she would have to get a cosmetology license because there weren't any esthetics programs by themselves. "I kept searching," reports Karin. "I found my school by looking in the yellow pages of the phone book. I saw the school at the end of the week, and it was all I could think about. I started school two weeks later, completed a 13-week, 450-hour program, and got the best base education I could ask for."

Estheticians must evaluate each client's skin through observation, testing, and discussion. Once the client's skin type and problems are identified, the esthetician proceeds with various treatments. These might include relaxing or stimulating massage, steam, heat, and light treatments, and the application of cleansers, peels, masks, toners, or astringents. Estheticians also use parrafin therapy, aromatherapy, hydrotherapy, and body scrubs, and apply waxing treatments to remove unwanted hair from face and body.

Karin Cadle gives a facial that lasts one hour and fifteen minutes. It includes consultation, cleansing, exfoliation, steam, a 30-minute facial and décolleté massage, a treatment mask tailored to the client's needs, hand and arm massage, extractions, and moisturizer and sunscreen application. She also does body treatments, waxing, and spa manicures and pedicures. The latter include scrubs and masks that treat the skin of the hands and feet.

Estheticians also advise women on the correct makeup formulations for their skin type and teach clients how to duplicate a professional makeup job at home. They advise clients on proper cleansing and care until the next visit. Clients might be invited to purchase from the salon the skin care and makeup products that will best suit their particular skin type.

You're On Your Way to Beautiful Skin if You...

1. Avoid sun exposure. Wear a sunscreen to ward off brown spots, tiny red spider veins, and premature lines.
2. Don't smoke. It makes lines around your lips and creates free radicals that break down collagen.
3. Don't pick pimples. You've heard it over and over because it's true. Picking can result in scarring and further infection.
4. Don't crash-diet. Your skin needs nutrients just like the rest of your body.
5. Don't use irritating products. Don't use anything that causes redness, irritation, or itching.

Estheticians work primarily in beauty salons, skin care clinics, and spas. Many choose to open their own skin care salons. Sheryl Baba worked in retail cosmetics for 15 years before she decided to go to school. "After helping thousands of customers with their skin care and makeup needs, I decided I needed to get my license in esthetics to realize my dream of owning my own salon. In the past three years, with the advantage of a state license, I have developed a profitable skin care business in my salon."

"I had no idea how broad the field of esthetics was until I went to a trade show in Miami, while I was still in school," says Karin Cadle. "What an eye opener! There are so many different avenues to take. You can be the person you want to be in this industry—esthetician, cosmetician, beauty therapist, practitioner, makeup artist, salesperson, cosmetic buyer, manufacturer's representative, spa owner, research and development—and the list goes on."

WHAT THE JOB IS *REALLY* LIKE

Jami Derr works a varied schedule, but she usually works Wednesday through Saturday, 31 hours a week. "I find that I can make as much money by consolidating my clients into four days, and I feel much more refreshed having a three-day weekend."

"An average day might be three eyebrow and/or lip waxes, one herbal exfoliation peel, two deep-cleansing facials, and one massage." (Jami also is trained as a massage therapist.) Some days she sees more clients, some days less.

"I sometimes come in early or stay late for certain clients, but I am the one to decide this. I can always arrange my work schedule to accommodate special occasions, vacations, and so on. I am very fortunate in that I have a week's paid vacation, and my employer pays the full amount for much of my continuing education."

Continuing education is part of the job for most estheticians, whether formal or not. Jami stays on top of what is going on in the esthetics field by reading and taking as many classes as possible. She subscribes to three professional skin care magazines, takes classes at every opportunity, and attends trade shows.

The rewards of the job are evident as customers who follow the recommended skin-care routines return, looking better and more confident with each visit.

A Person
Who's Done It

VITAL STATISTICS

Six years ago, when Jami Derr, 31, became very ill with a painful, itchy skin rash from head to toe, she had no idea it would lead her to a satisfying career in esthetics.

I went from doctor to doctor with no relief from this horrible rash. Then I began seeing a naturopathic doctor and learned about alternative/holistic therapies. From that point on I became very interested in herbs, supplements, and alternative therapies. I had my first introduction to massage when my doctor recommended lymphatic drainage massage. Over the next three years I slowly regained my health. I wanted to get into the holistic health field, and completed a 500-hour program to become a certified massage therapist. I began working part time in the salon where I work now.

My employer couldn't find an esthetician for the salon, and asked if I would be interested in studying for an esthetician's license. At the time, I didn't really appreciate the value of skin care, but I went ahead and signed up for school. It was an hour's drive to the school and an hour back, and that wasn't easy, especially on the days I worked. I graduated after six months with a cosmetician's license, but I was not really satisfied with the training I had received, and by that time I had grown to really enjoy skin care. I wanted to learn more than just the basics.

Fortunately, a friend told me about Esthe-Tec school in Philadelphia, and I began taking continuing education classes. The classes helped me get up and running with skin care, and now my job is extremely rewarding. When I go home at night I feel really good about myself and what I do. My clients are varied and I deal with many different skin types. I see young teens who are just starting to have a few breakouts, and full-blown acne in both teenagers and adults. I work on special problems such as hyperpigmentation and rosacea. Many of my mature clients are looking for antiaging treatments. I would say they make up between 50 and 60 percent of my clientele. I perform chemical peels, and herbal exfoliation peels, and am in the process of purchasing a microdermabrasion machine. I also do waxing and makeup application.

It is wonderful to have the opportunity to help clients achieve their skin care goals, but there is more to the job than that. Clients share very personal things with me as I get to know them, and I always strive to say at least one thing to boost each client's self-esteem. It's kind of ironic, but it's good to help people see that they are wonderful "under the skin."

As for the future, I am going to take an aromatherapy course in a few months, and then I plan to start a Wellness Consultant program. I would like to eventually start a Wellness Clinic and Advanced Skin Care school in my area.

GETTING IN AND MOVING UP

Esthetics is a field that has just begun to gain tremendous popularity. As the field grows, new esthetics schools will open. For now, it may take some digging to find out what you need for licensure and to find a good school. Check with your state board of cosmetology to determine the regulations in your state. Most courses take between 10 and 14 weeks, and comprise 300 to 400 hours.

Once you have your license, whether it is in cosmetology or in an esthetics specialty, your best teacher will be hands-on experience and networking with other estheticians to share information. Taking continuing education classes will teach you more about skin care and you will also meet other estheticians and make contacts that may prove valuable later on. As in other careers within the cosmetology field, patience is required while you build a client base. "It takes time," advises Jami Derr. "But if you are honest and diligent, it will come."

Treating Clients

"I treat my clients the way I would want to be treated, and if I sense a particular need due to something they say or their response to a treatment, I try to act on it and go the extra mile. I send birthday, thank you, and holiday cards with discounts for future services. I've gotten flowers for my clients for Teacher Appreciation Day and Secretary's Day. It's the little things that count and keep them coming back."

Karin Cadle

EMPLOYMENT FORECAST

Esthetics is one of the fastest growing areas of cosmetology; in fact, it is virtually exploding. Many in the industry attribute this to the aging of "baby boomers," who are willing to pay for the professional advice and care estheticians can offer. Because of the increasing demand, a growing number of salons are offering skin care services, and they are having a difficult time finding estheticians with skills beyond the basic.

Because the esthetics industry is always changing and growing, continuing and advanced training are necessary for a number of services offered by estheticians, such as lymphatic drainage, chemical peels, and specialized makeup work. In addition, estheticians are often employed by dermatologists and plastic surgeons to assist in certain treatment procedures.

EARNINGS

Statistics on the average earnings of estheticians are not widely available since they are grouped in with cosmetologists. The Cosmetology Advancement Foundation lists $32,000 as the average cosmetologist's yearly earnings, and it is reasonable to think that this figure would hold true for estheticians as well. Experience, the area in which they practice, the number of hours they work, and the number and class of clients they serve are all factors that influence estheticians' earnings.

PROFESSIONAL CONNECTIONS

Aesthetics International Association has been involved with the industry's growth for more than 25 years. It sponsors workshops and seminars at conferences and symposiums, and is involved in legislation and certification issues. The association publishes its own newsletter, and a section of *Dermascope* magazine is devoted to AIA news and industry-related articles.

The American Society of Esthetic Medicine aims to provide resources to those involved in the rapidly growing field of medical esthetics and to define the role of the esthetician in the healthcare industry.

FOR INFORMATION, CONTACT:

Aesthetics International Association
2611 North Beltline Road, Suite 140
Sunnyvale, TX 75182
Phone: (972) 203-8530
Fax: (972) 203-8754
Web site: *http://www.beautyworks.com/aia*

American Society of Esthetic Medicine
3901 East Livingston Avenue, Suite 102
Columbus, OH 43227
Phone: (614) 239-9000
Web site: *http://www.beautyworks.com/asem*

RESOURCES

Dermascope
3939 East Highway 80, Suite 408
Mesquite, TX 75150

Skin, Inc.
362 South Schmale Road
Carol Stream, IL 60188-2787

A FEW KEY POINTS TO REMEMBER:

- Estheticians specialize in care of the skin.
- Basic skin care is part of a cosmetology license, but advanced and continuing education are necessary for success.
- Estheticians must have patience to develop a base of clientele.
- Estheticians need to be good listeners and make people feel better on the inside as well as the outside.

CHAPTER FIVE

Nail Technician

What do millions of modern women have in common with women who lived 4,000 years ago?

Fingernail decoration. Manicuring supplies have been found in ancient Egyptian tombs. Once a luxury for the wealthy, professional manicures are now affordable and immensely popular.

They go by different names in different places: manicurist, nail technician, nail artist, nail professional, and nail specialist. What they all have in common is that they are part of a business that began to boom in the 1980s. Millions of American women now have their nails done every ten days to two weeks, and while the average price of a natural nail manicure averages out to only $13, artificial nails average about $40 per salon visit.

Based on studies and estimates done by *Nails Magazine*, American women spend almost six and a half *billion* dollars annually on manicures, pedicures, and artificial nails, a figure that does not include tips given to nail techs or purchases of nail supplies. From 1991 to 1997, the number of nail salons in

America nearly doubled from 26,752 to 45,163, according to Vi Nelson, a spokesperson for the Nail Manufacturer's Council.

THE RIGHT STUFF

"Some people might think nail technicians are people who couldn't 'make it' in other professions," notes Kathy Kirkland, Executive Editor of *Nailpro*, "but that's far from the truth. I know nail techs who used to be scientists or in other professions, but they loved *having* their nails done and were encouraged to become techs.

"Nail techs are 'people persons'; they enjoy other people and know the benefits of touching and servicing others. And it's also a profession that can be very lucrative. It's a great profession, and the people in it are caring, friendly, and wonderful."

Nail techs must be able to produce a quality set of nails quickly. Organization, professionalism, and impeccable appearance are essential, and nail techs must be good listeners.

While cosmetology classes provide training in nails, and many cosmetologists are doing nails in addition to or instead of other services, two-thirds of the respondents to a 1998 survey conducted by *Nailpro* reported that they had obtained the nail tech license alone and did nails exclusively.

State regulations concerning licenses for nail technicians vary widely. For example, in Arkansas, Kentucky, Oklahoma, Oregon, Tennessee, and Texas, 600 hours are required for a nail technician's license, yet Iowa requires only 40. Four states—Alaska, Utah, Connecticut, and Nebraska—have no separate licensing requirements.

Here is a breakdown for a typical curriculum of 350 clock hours:

- 85 hours in Practical Application

- 30 hours in Business Practice

- 220 hours in Practice and Procedures

- 15 hours in Concepts

The types of courses vary from state to state, but you should learn the laws and rules of your state as they affect cosmetology, basic sanitation, sterilization and safety procedures, and enough about nail disorders and diseases to be able to recognize which problems you should and should not attempt to treat. Basic business training is also extremely helpful, since more than half of nail techs either rent space in a salon or own their own businesses.

The minimum goal of any school should be to prepare you to pass the state licensing exam. Beyond that, look for national accreditation, state licensing, and courses that instill good work habits, teach you how to act ethically and professionally, and encourage your own individual creative style. Depending on the hours required, and whether you enroll full time or part time, you may need as little as ten weeks or up to six months to complete the coursework.

After that, keep learning. Take an interest in what other nail technicians are doing. Gina Wallace, a highly successful nail technician who travels all over the world educating other nail techs, encourages new graduates to find mentors to help them in the business.

WHAT NAIL TECHNICIANS DO

Nail technicians' basic services include manicures and pedicures, acrylic and gel nails, and nail art. They also give hand and arm massages, and apply exfoliation and paraffin treatments, hand and foot masks, and conditioners. An additional source of income for nail techs is selling professional products for between-visits maintenance or treating a particular problem such as dry cuticles.

Independent Survey

An independent survey conducted by *Nailpro* (December 1998) showed that 30 percent of nail techs worked in full-service salons, 27 percent in a nails-only salon, and 25 percent in a salon offering hair and nail services. Most of the remaining respondents worked in salons offering nails and tanning, nails and skin care, or at day spas.

WHAT THE JOB IS *REALLY* LIKE

A fully booked nail technician can serve about 35 clients per week, but most do not book that many. *Nails* found the average work week for a nail technician to be 32 hours. Many are raising families or have additional jobs.

Like most jobs, nail technology has its drawbacks. When *Nails* held discussions with technicians about job satisfaction, a group of California techs agreed that they enjoyed being needed and providing a service that made people feel great, but they found their roles as amateur "therapists and marriage counselors" sometimes a little too intense.

Technicians also had complaints about unfair competition, too many inadequately trained workers entering the profession, lack of benefits, and health concerns related to breathing fumes from the chemicals in nail products, carpal tunnel syndrome, and back problems.

There are several ways nail technicians, like stylists, are compensated. A tech may work as an employee in a salon for a small salary plus tips and commission on products, work in a salon on a commission-only basis, or rent space in a salon, with fees, tips, and profit on products as the source of income. Good records of income and retail sales must be kept, and quarterly income tax returns filed. Techs may be required to collect and remit state sales tax on the products they sell.

Owners of nail salons make more money on the average than salon employees or booth renters, but they also have more headaches. If what you really love is doing nails, you may find yourself spending more time than you would like to on paperwork, employee management, rent collection, and worrying about things like advertising and insurance. Some of these problems can be avoided if you opt to open a "one tech" (yourself) salon.

A Person
Who's Done It

MEET DONNA MARIE AMADORI-TUCKER

VITAL STATISTICS

When Donna Marie Amadori-Tucker, 41, a former fitness instructor, was in cosmetology school, there were times she wondered if it was really a career she wanted to pursue. She had a teacher who encouraged her, and today she is in business for herself and couldn't be happier.

I recently opened Le Beautique Salon in Blasdell, New York. I offer waxing services, artificial nails, natural manicures, and pedicures. Soon I will be offering hair services. I am so glad I completed the entire education in cosmetology rather than just getting the nail specialty license. I am not limited in what I can offer, and there are many more doors open to me.

As important as a good school is, I think the training you get when you finish school counts the most. If you work as an intern or assistant at the best salon you can when you first leave school, you will be getting invaluable experience every day. While you are in school, you usually do a short internship in a salon. With that opportunity to build a good rapport, you have a good chance of returning there after you are licensed to work. Low-budget salons do not teach you anything about advancement.

I cherish the friendships I have developed and appreciate the loyalty of my dedicated customers, but even so, "burnout" can occur when you work a lot of hours. I often work from 10:00 A.M. until 9:00 P.M. Of course, since I am in business for myself, I'm able to schedule breaks to fit in the demands of my family—but often I do work straight through. Sometimes, clients can get a little too demanding when you give too much, but you can't forget that you have a life of your own. It's a matter of keeping a balance between your work routine and the rest of your life. Some weeks are slow, and that gives you time to recuperate.

I have made a specialty of offering my services to handicapped people, and that is one of the greatest joys of my job. They need to know that they are special and beautiful, and the thing is, they really *are*. I can give them gorgeous nails, and while I'm doing that, I have constant eye contact and physical touch. Lots of people they encounter look away or don't want to touch them.

One client in particular has been a real inspiration to me. For a number of years she came to see me, and I always enjoyed her appointments. She is a sweet person, and although unable to have children, she is a devoted "mom" to her pets. Over the years, her physical abilities began to deteriorate. She had developed multiple sclerosis. At first, she just needed help getting into and out of her vehicle at the salon. By about a year ago, she had come to rely on a little scooter to get around. I knew she had financial troubles because of the high expense of experimental drugs for this disease, yet she never complained. What a beautiful person she is to smile and love life without a complaint! Today, I go to her home to do her nails. She likes to have her eyebrows waxed, too. She greets me at the door on her scooter, and when I leave her home I know I made her life a little easier—and she makes mine richer because of her courage and her positive attitude.

A number of my clients confide in me, and I make a point of really listening. It means a lot to them if I remember that they are going through a difficult divorce or having a problem with one of their children. They just want to talk about it to someone who cares, and just by listening to them I know I am helping.

GETTING IN AND MOVING UP

Beginning nail technicians must be patient while building a clientele. Salon owners are often reluctant to rent booth space to beginners because they have no customers, so new techs often start as salon employees. "Building a book," that is, filling as many available spaces as possible with clients who will return for standing appointments, is an important goal for beginning techs.

Gina Wallace has these suggestions for increasing business: "Get some attractive business cards. Distribute flyers at PTA meetings, church events, local rallies, and so forth. Offer to do a free first set of nails for the clerks at the cosmetic counters at the mall. Don't forget to leave them a pile of your business cards to distribute, and offer them a discount for every referral who books an appointment."

Gina adds that quantity is wasted effort if the client doesn't re-book. "Quality is the name of the game here. Clients who receive quality will travel distances, sacrifice lunch hours, and cancel social events to make their appointments on time!"

Dee Manieri, a North Carolina technician who has been doing nails for 14 years, says working in a full-service salon has definite advantages for beginning techs. If you work in a nail salon, everyone there is trying to build a nail clientele.

In a full-service salon, you can help one another. The massage therapist can recommend a spa pedicure to her client, for example, while the nail technician, who massages only her client's arms and hands, might suggest a full-body massage. "You have to make it happen," says Dee. "You don't walk out of nail school and into a $50,000 a year job. You have to be dependable and look and act professional."

Getting and Keeping Clientele

Donna Marie Amadori-Tucker shares these tips for getting and keeping clientele:

1. Always smile and LISTEN to your clients. Remember the hand and the heart work together and that's where you build a reltionship with trust. You hold their hand for a good portion of an hour every other week. That is a bond!

2. Confidence is very important. What they tell you is like talking to their therapist.

3. Treat them once in a while to a luxury like a hand massage or free nail art. They need to know that they are special and that you appreciate their business.

4. "The Buddy System." Have them send you a client and give them both a break in the price. It works better than advertising and is much cheaper.

5. Always educate your clients on new information. There are always new disorders and diseases. A good nail tech stays on top of things.

6. Remember, you have the power to make them feel good about their appearance and themselves.

Experienced nail technicians say they stay on top of trends and techniques by continuing to take classes, reading trade magazines, and attending trade shows. Another way to learn is to network on-line with other nail professionals. Join a chat room or connect with others in your field by e-mail.

You can boost your entry-level income by polishing up your sales skills. For inspiration, try reading a book on salesmanship, or attend a marketing class. Remember that doing the best work you can reflects well on you and your profession. It also provides another benefit that will help you fill your appointment book; every client is a walking, gesturing advertisement for your work!

EMPLOYMENT FORECAST

According to the *Nails* survey cited earlier, there were 48,085 nail salons at the beginning of 1999—3,300 more than a year before. The Bureau of Labor Statistics projects a growth of 44.7 percent for manicurists from 1996 through 2006. Nail technology continues to be one of the fastest-growing segments of the cosmetology field. For the technician who is skilled in the latest procedures and willing to learn as new trends develop, it is a job seeker's market.

EARNINGS

Nailpro's 1998 survey found the average salary of a nail tech to be $23,357. Those in the business less than three years averaged just over $16,000, while those who had been working 7 to 14 years averaged nearly twice that, $31,972. *Nails* found a tech's average annual income to be $23,462. As the *Nails* survey points out, earnings are affected by experience, where you live, the prices you charge, and how many clients you see each week. Nail techs in the top 10 percent income bracket ($50,000 or more a year) work longer hours, see more clients, and have been doing nails much longer.

PROFESSIONAL CONNECTIONS

Nails Industry Association
2512 Artesia Boulevard
Redondo Beach, CA 90278
Phone: (800) 846-2457

American Association of Cosmetology Schools
15825 North 71st Street, Suite 100
Scottsdale, AZ 85254
Phone: (800) 831-1086

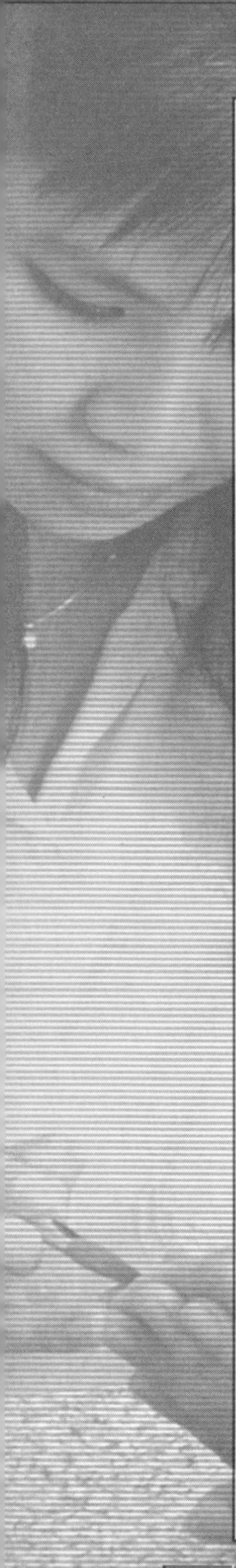

RESOURCES

American Salon Magazine
270 Madison Avenue
New York, NY 10016
Web site: *http://hairnet.com*

Modern Salon Magazine
P.O. Box 1414
Lincolnshire, IL 60069

Nailpro Magazine
7628 Densmore Avenue
Van Nuys, CA 91406-2042
Phone: (818) 782-7328
Web site: *http://www.nailpro.com*

Nails Magazine
21061 S. Western Avenue
Torrance, CA 90501
Phone: (310) 533-2400
Web site: *http://nailsmag.com*

A FEW KEY POINTS TO REMEMBER

- American women spend billions of dollars each year on manicures, pedicures, and artificial nails.
- Nail technology is one of the fastest-growing fields in cosmetology.
- Nail technicians are "people persons," who enjoy working with others.
- In most states, you can get a separate nail specialty license and do not have to complete cosmetology school.
- Nail technicians give manicures and pedicures, do acrylic and gel nails, and give hand and arm massages and other treatments.
- As a nail technician, you must be scrupulous about sterilizing equipment.

CHAPTER SIX

Makeup Artist

The next time you go to a movie, look at the credits at the end. You'll notice at least one makeup artist listed, probably a team of professionals. You'll find makeup artists behind the scenes at television studios, theaters, modeling studios, catalog shoots, magazines, and fashion shows. Celebrities and politicians employ makeup artists to help them present their best faces to the public.

These are some of the high-profile jobs, but the talents of makeup artists are now available to everyone. Makeup artists work at salons and day spas, at department stores, and at glamour photography studios—all affordable for the middle-class American woman.

You can even find makeup artists in the medical field, working with victims of disfiguring accidents, plastic surgery patients, and dermatology patients. Corrective makeup techniques taught by specialists can go a long way toward boosting self-esteem. David Nicholas is a very special makeup artist who for years has volunteered his time at the Shriners Burn Institute in Boston. Through his art, he has created the illusion of smoother skin and more regular features for courageous burn survivors.

THE RIGHT STUFF

Makeup artists work directly with the public, so they must be friendly and tactful. Most people are very sensitive and self-conscious about how they look. Successful makeup artists know how to make people feel as beautiful inside as they look on the outside.

It is helpful to have a talent for teaching since the customer will be expected to follow through with the skin care regimen prescribed by the makeup artist and be able to apply her new makeup herself.

Finally, makeup artists must have a steady hand and a good eye for detail. Makeup artistry is an area where perfectionism is an asset.

WHAT MAKEUP ARTISTS DO

Makeup artists begin with an analysis of the skin. They start out with a clean canvas, and for the makeup artist, this means properly cleansed skin. He or she needs to be able to clearly define what type of skin the customer has—dry, oily, normal, combination, or sensitive.

Cleansers come in many different formulations appropriate for different skin types. Cleansing is followed by a toner or astringent that removes residue and refines pores, and finally, a moisturizer is used. The makeup artist determines which types of these products are best for the client's skin and demonstrates their use.

You have probably seen enough before-and-after pictures to know how much a face can be changed with makeup application. Women may choose colors simply because they look pretty at the cosmetic counter rather than considering how those colors will look on them. Makeup artists are trained to study the client's face and choose colors that will enhance individual traits.

Makeup artists use highlighting and shadowing to alter the contours of the face. For example, a wide nose can be made to appear slimmer if the bridge and center are highlighted with a lighter color or foundation, while the sides are shaded with a darker color. Cheekbones can be "brought out" with lighter colors and a touch of blush. Dark circles, scars, broken capillaries, and other small blemishes can be covered with concealer. Makeup artists test many foundation colors until just the right one is found, the color that disappears into the customer's skin, leaving the complexion smooth and flawless.

Eyes become more vibrant with the application of eyeliner, eyeshadow, and mascara. The makeup artist has the skill to apply products so that eyes can be made to look closer together, farther apart, rounder, larger, less deep-set, and so forth. Makeup artists know how to even out an uneven lip line, plump up too-thin lips, and choose just the right lip colors.

Makeup Tips from the Pros

1. When you line the eye, start at the outside corner and come in halfway. Then go from the inside corner to the middle to meet the first line.
2. Use a light or neutral concealer as your eye shadow base. It will make shadow last longer.
3. If you have time to apply only one thing, make it lipstick. It does more to brighten your face than any other cosmetic.
4. A spot of lighter lipstick in the middle of your lips will make them appear fuller.

WHAT THE JOB IS *REALLY* LIKE

"In my freelance business as a makeup artist, I'm on location for weddings, professional photo shoots, and fashion shows," says Sheryl Baba, a licensed esthetician and makeup artist in Cummaquid, Massachusetts. "I have worked with hundreds of brides, models, and celebrities in the resort area where I live. It sounds glamorous, but it's a lot of hard work. You must put yourself in a marketing position to attract these jobs, and you have to be talented, professional, and prepared. You have to network with the right people, and always remember that the client is the star and you are only a member of the supporting cast.

"Three days a week, I'm at my salon doing facials, spa body therapies, makeup, waxing—and being the best team player I can be. My day at the salon begins at about 9:30 A.M. I look over my appointment book to see who's coming in and for what services. I must be completely organized and have all my products ready to go and my tools clean.

"Most appointments are scheduled on the hour or the half hour. Spa or salon time is different from real time. An hour facial is usually 45 minutes of treatment. That gives my client six minutes to undress and take off her jewelry before the treatment. Afterwards, she has six minutes to get dressed and leave the room. That leaves me three precious minutes to prepare the room for the next client, who is already waiting! When you are part of a package of services, for example 'A Day of Beauty,' you must know who receives the guest next and not keep that beauty technician waiting.

"I love to perform facials. I set the scene in my facial room with soft music, aromatherapy, candlelight, and plush textures. To help a client unwind, de-stress, and finally see an improvement in her complexion is deeply rewarding. The results are doubled when the client commits to the recommended home care and regular treatments.

"When I have a 'full book' I usually bring my lunch and eat it on the run. I am usually booked until 6 P.M. or later. If I have any open time, I try to assist customers in the retail center. It is a good place to generate sales and future bookings."

A Person
Who's Done It

VITAL STATISTICS

Always intrigued by the fashion and beauty business, Sheryl Baba, 37, took a short makeup course just for fun. Her instructor felt she showed promise, and suggested she go into cosmetics at the retail level. That was step one toward a rewarding and exciting career.

During my career in retail I had the opportunity to work for some of the most famous cosmetics companies in the world. I enjoyed the financial security of being employed by the department store, with an hourly rate plus commission and health benefits. I was intensively trained in skin care and makeup techniques, product ingredients, and customer service.

I had hundreds of faces to "play makeup" on and refine my skills. Women love to see themselves reinvented from someone else's point of view. Through my contacts at the counter, I was able to market myself as a makeup artist for weddings, fashion shows, photo shoots, and lectures. I volunteered to lecture for local women's groups and do makeup for fashion shows just to get my name in the program credits. The store I represented saw the value in this exposure and would often donate a basket of products to raffle. I was very fortunate that the cosmetic department manager supported my efforts. Soon I was being invited to the most popular social and professional gatherings to demonstrate my products and bring those customers back to the counter.

But retail is what it is: big business; fast-paced; nights, weekends, and holidays required; sales goals; pressure; and much more. I was always late to the Christmas Eve party and never much fun on Thanksgiving because I dreaded the next day—retail's busiest of the year. I wouldn't have missed it for the world, though. I love to do makeup and help other women to see the beauty in themselves.

Through all this, I knew I would never be happy until I had my own makeup studio. In the state of Massachusetts, you must be board-certified and licensed in skin care to do makeup outside a retail organization. So three years ago I went back to the Elizabeth Grady School of Esthetics, where I first took that short makeup course, and became a licensed esthetician.

My concept of special occasion makeup comes from studying hundreds of classic black-and-white movie stills of such beauty icons as Grace Kelly, Audrey Hepburn, and Marilyn Monroe. These are women who have defined classic beauty, glamour, and femininity. In these photos a certain look is represented without any obvious cosmetics. You see only healthy skin, good bone structure, and light and shadows. It is endless style. I use well-blended shades in the client's own innate color palette, and when my client views her photos 10 or 20 years from now, she will not look outdated, but will retain that classically beautiful look.

Having my license and state board approval has also afforded me other opportunities. I work at my salon three days a week, and the flexible schedule I enjoy has allowed me to work for several professional makeup companies as an educator, artist, consultant, and platform demonstrator. I have traveled all over the East Coast, working booths for major beauty, esthetic, and spa shows next to the presidents and creators of the major companies. These shows offer continuing education classes on the most advanced facial, spa, and makeup techniques taught by leaders in this industry.

Our field has long been considered a luxury and a frivolous expense. As technology gives us new and more effective advancements in skin care products, and as cosmetics straddle the line between cover-up and treatment, we can offer our clients services that truly make a difference in their complexions, in their self-confidence, and in their lives.

I share my career here so that others may be inspired to join me in this exciting and rewarding field. It's necessary to take chances, to learn from your mistakes, to help others see their own beauty, and to always remember that life is the journey, not the destination!

(Note: Sheryl Baba invites those interested in the esthetics/makeup artistry field to e-mail her at *sbaba1@aol.com.*)

GETTING IN AND MOVING UP

In cosmetology school, a certain number of school hours are set aside for instruction in skin analysis and makeup. If you are interested solely in makeup, you can get an esthetician's license and then take as many continuing education classes as you can. Theatrical makeup and camouflage makeup are advanced courses that can be completed in as little as a week or two. The more education you have, the more opportunities will be open to you.

Many cosmetic companies train their employees in skin care and makeup, as Sheryl Baba's employer did. While this training does not lead to licensing, it is a good way to find out how interested you are in pursuing the field further. If you are still in high school, you might want to get a part-time job in the cosmetics area of a department or drugstore. If you find you enjoy the work, consider getting your full cosmetologist's license or the esthetics specialty (see Chapter Four).

To succeed, you must enjoy helping others to feel better about themselves and be comfortable touching them and interacting with them. You must be creative and secure in promoting yourself and your services. It will take patience to build your business, whether you work for a salon or for yourself.

EMPLOYMENT FORECAST

As the number of beauty salons, day spas, and wellness centers grows, so does the demand for estheticians and makeup artists. As in other areas of cosmetology, the large population of aging baby boomers is increasing the demand for services.

The possibilities for advancement as a makeup artist are wide open. You've probably heard of Kevin Aucoin, Bobbi Brown, and Trish McEvoy. They started at the bottom too.

EARNINGS

As a makeup artist, your income will depend on your own effort. If you start out at a department store, you will receive an hourly wage and probably commission on what you sell. If you work in a salon, you will most likely work on commission or rent space from the salon.

"If your least expensive service is a lip wax at $10, and your most expensive facial is $65, you could consider your average hourly rate $37.50. If you are splitting 50-50 with the salon, that's $18.75 an hour for you," explains Sheryl Baba. "But remember, that is only if you are fully booked."

As a freelance makeup artist, you can set your own rates. You may charge by the day, the half-day, or the hour.

"Experience, professional reputation, tear sheets, and film credits will enable you to move up the ranks and command more money for your time," notes Sheryl, whose on-location prices for a bridal party start at $60 per person, with a minimum of two people.

PROFESSIONAL CONNECTIONS

Aesthetics International Association
2611 North Beltline Road, Suite 140
Sunnyvale, TX 75182
Phone: (972) 203-8530
Fax: (972) 203-8754
Web site: *http://www.beautyworks.com/aia*

American Beauty Association
401 North Michigan Avenue
Chicago, IL 60611
Phone: (800) 868-4265
Web site: *http://www.americanbeauty.org*

National Cosmetology Association
401 North Michigan Avenue
Chicago, IL 60611
Phone: (312) 644-6610
Web site: *http://NCA-now.com*

RESOURCES

MAGAZINES

Makeup Artist
P.O. Box 4316
Sunland, CA 91041-4316
Phone: (818) 404-6770
Web site: *http://www.makeupmag.com*

1st Hold
Set the Pace Publishing Group
4237 Los Nietos Drive
Los Angeles, CA 90027-2911
Phone: (323) 913-0773
Web site: *http://www.setthepacepubgroup.com*

Les Nouvelles Esthetiques
306 Alcazar Avenue, Suite 204
Coral Gables, FL 33134
Phone: (800) 471-0229
Web site: *http://www.lneonline.com*

WEB SITES

http://www.makeupmania.com

http://www.cosmeticconnection.com

http://www.profaces.com

A FEW KEY POINTS TO REMEMBER

• Makeup artists work in the entertainment industry, for public figures, modeling agencies, magazines, photography studios, weddings, and other special events.

• They also help people who are disfigured appear more normal and provide skin care and makeup advice to the average person.

• To pursue a career as a freelance makeup artist, begin by obtaining an esthetics license.

• Theatrical and corrective makeup require advanced training.

CHAPTER SEVEN

Permanent Cosmetic Technician

I magine waking up looking as if you have just applied eyeliner, eyebrow pencil, and lipstick. The art of permanent cosmetic makeup has made this possible for thousands of busy women. Cosmetologists and others trained to perform the procedures are finding lucrative careers in this fast-growing field.

Permanent cosmetic makeup is also called cosmetic tattooing, dermapigmentation, microimplantation, micropigmentation, and permanent makeup. It involves applying permanent pigment under the skin with a needle, and is basically the same process used in traditional artistic tattooing. The most common procedures are eyeliner, eyebrows, and lipliner, but full lip color, lash enhancement, and cheek blush are also possible and growing in popularity.

Permanent makeup may sound like the height of vanity to some, but it has many applications. Those with poor eyesight, contact lenses, or unsteady hands can save hours of frustration, and know they always look their best. The handicapped, those with allergies to cosmetics, and people who have disfiguring scars due to injuries or surgery benefit as well.

Gaining in Popularity

Permanent Makeup began to gain popularity in the late 1970s, when tattoo artists started offering it to their customers. When cosmetologists became interested, training programs appeared everywhere. The industry began to grow rapidly and continues to do so today.

THE RIGHT STUFF

At the present time, only half of U.S. states regulate permanent cosmetics. In these states, information is included in the regulations governing tattooing. While there is a move toward uniform licensing requirements, it is largely up to those practicing in the field to govern themselves. Permanent cosmetic technicians must understand, above all, the importance of thorough training. With the promise of "big bucks" down the road to lure students in, there are many expensive, but inadequate, training programs available. Some offer only one or two days of class, often with no hands-on training. Permanent cosmetics are just that—*permanent*. A person's appearance, the face he or she presents to the world, is altered forever by permanent makeup.

In 1990 Susan Church and Susan Preston established the Society of Permanent Cosmetic Professionals, a nonprofit organization that sets guidelines for training and standards for the profession. The Society suggests that anyone considering a career in permanent cosmetics should evaluate several programs very carefully before deciding which one will provide the best beginning training. A beginning program should not claim to train the student to do any more than eyeliner, eyebrows, and lipliner. Full lip color and blush require advanced training, and corrective pigment camouflage calls for even more instruction. In a good training program, there should be no more than four students per teacher, and the student should complete several procedures in class before offering his or her services to the public. For hands-on training, the Society of Permanent Cosmetic Professionals requires a one-on-one student-teacher ratio. Ideally, a school should have at least 40 hours of education, hands-on application, follow-up guidance, and instructor accessibility to answer questions after the student begins practicing.

At the International Institute of Permanent Cosmetics in Fountain Valley, California, students devote 40 hours to home study of videos and printed material before they enter the classroom/lab setting. There they spend an additional 40 hours of intensive training that covers sterilization, sanitation, anatomy, consultation, various techniques, before and after care, and even marketing, business, and goal-setting. The Institute also offers lifelong technical support for its students.

On course completion, students may immediately start working on clients. "It is best to work on friends and family," advises Susan Church, Education Director. "A technician who is not confident after training should ask to apprentice with an experienced technician."

Permanent cosmetic technicians must know and abide by OSHA and Centers for Disease Control safety standards. They must maintain spotless facilities, and must be clean and neat themselves. Because people who undergo permanent cosmetic procedures are understandably nervous, it is helpful to have a positive, reassuring, and compassionate manner.

WHAT PERMANENT COSMETIC TECHNICIANS DO

Permanent cosmetic technicians use three techniques (or "modalities"):
1. the coil machine
2. the rotary machine
3. the hand method ("manual tool").

The choice of which method to use is up to the technician. Each uses sterile disposable needles.

For male clients, technicians can improve the appearance of bald spots, give them fuller eyebrows, and simulate a beard on scarred facial skin. The properly trained permanent cosmetic technician can also camouflage body tattoos for those who no longer want them, for instance, young people who have liberated themselves from gangs.

An eyebrow procedure may mean total creation of eyebrows or simply filling in areas that tend to be sparse. Eyeliner may be a natural-looking enhancement that is not at all noticeable to a more defined line, depending on the customer's choice. Lipliner can give more definition, correct uneven lips, or add fullness to the mouth. Full lip color may be applied in a natural tone or a brighter color.

Highly trained permanent cosmetic technicians also work with surgeons, using corrective pigment camouflage techniques for scarring from injuries, surgery, or variations in skin pigmentation. After a mastectomy and reconstructive surgery, permanent cosmetic technicians can recreate a natural-looking areola, and can even give the illusion of a protruding nipple.

WHAT THE JOB IS *REALLY* LIKE

When a client contacts a permanent cosmetic technician, the first step is a consultation, which lasts about 20 minutes. Technicians maintain portfolios of before-and-after photos so clients can see examples of the available procedures and the effects of each. The client and technician discuss desires and expectations; then the client's medical history is taken, as well as a "before" photo. It is important to address all of the client's questions and concerns at the consultation. Necessary paperwork is completed and consent forms are signed.

On the day of the procedure, a topical anesthetic is applied to minimize discomfort. The pigment is applied using single-use sterile needles. Following the procedure, the client receives aftercare instructions. Complete healing takes four to six weeks. The client then returns for a touch-up procedure, similar to the first.

"The average day of a serious full-time technician may consist of one to three client consultations and three to four procedure applications," says Susan. "The technician's daily challenges may include dealing with high-risk clients, inappropriate client color choices, improper makeup placement, and client apprehension. The technician may also face challenges from clients whose brows have turned purple or pink, lips that have turned blue or black, eyeliner that has migrated under the skin, or corrective pigment camouflage applications that do not match. Beginning technicians should not undertake these applications unless they are specifically trained to correct them"

A Person Who's Done It

MEET SUSAN CHURCH

VITAL STATISTICS

After working as a hairstylist for 20 years, Susan Church, 48, expanded into permanent cosmetics. Today she has her own clinic and school, is the author of several books and 12 technical videos, travels all over the world teaching and lecturing, and is one of the most highly regarded professionals in the field. Susan is a great example of how far a person can go with a cosmetology license, a lot of hard work, and a generous dose of compassion. Here's how she did it.

I was fortunate to have been exposed to a beauty salon setting from a very early age at my two aunts' salon in Copley, Ohio. I went to work with them when I was quite young. I'd talk to clients, take out rollers, sweep up hair, and so on. I learned at this early age about self-esteem and how looking better affects a person's psyche. I took cosmetology in high school, then worked at the May Company beauty salon in Akron, Ohio, to build clientele. I opened my first salon when I was in my early twenties.

When I first heard about permanent cosmetics I knew it would solve many problems for the traditional makeup client. The most common request that we heard in the salon was "Please be careful while shampooing my hair. Don't wash off my eyebrows." Clients would even hold towels over their faces to protect their drawn-on eyebrows.

Owning a salon and having employees depending on me to make money was a big responsibility. I would work ten to twelve hours, five or six days a week. Permanent cosmetic makeup seemed like a great addition to my full-service salon. When other salons were closed on Mondays, we were open and capitalized on it. This would be the perfect day to apply permanent makeup.

I took a two-day class and learned basically how to hold the machine, and how to market PCM (permanent cosmetic makeup). I knew just enough to be *very dangerous*. There were over 40 people in my class, with no hands-on application. Being a model, makeup artist, and cosmetologist for 20 years, I knew that PCM was not an exact science, but rather an art that needed to be fine-tuned. I learned most of my application techniques by trial and error.

My first client had absolutely no brow hair. I created the perfect brow for her. It complimented her facial features beautifully. I began her application and three hours later I had a client with red swollen skin, very little color, and dots in her brows. I had two bent needles and a sore back. She came back in two weeks and I proceeded to recreate that same brow over again. Her skin was still very tender to the touch. Being a willing participant in this whole adventure, she trusted me to complete her brows. Each application yielded a subtle shadow of color. After numerous touch-ups, I finally figured out proper protocol. Every hair designer will tell you about his or her first haircut or permanent wave disaster. That is the category in which I place my first PCM client.

As I learned more, my reputation as an expert in the industry grew. I wrote my first educational manual six months after my initial class. It was very detailed in the proper application of eyeliner, eyebrow hair simulation, and lipliner. I fielded, on average, 30 to 50 phone calls daily from students who just could not make PCM "work." I decided to start writing down the most common questions. There were over 300! It took me ten years to write, rewrite, and publish *Permanent Cosmetics A to Z, Basic and Advanced Fundamentals in the Art of Permanent Cosmetic Makeup*. This book has become a best-seller for PCM technicians.

I also wrote the Fourth Edition of *A Medical, Surgical, Tattoo Glossary*, with over 26 pages of terms and definitions, and *Permanent Cosmetics for the Consumer*, questions and answers for potential clients, with 16 pages of full-color before-and-after photos of all procedures. Like many people, I am a "visual" learner. I decided to film all of my procedures and make educational videos. To date, I have 12 educational videos utilizing both the coil and rotary machine.

Before long, schools were phoning me and asking me to teach for them. Most of the people who taught classes did not know the first thing about proper hands-on application. I was put in charge of The Instructor Assistance Line for thousands of students. I had to problem-solve with the "school of hard knocks" information that I had learned on my own.

In 1990 Susan Preston and I cofounded a nonprofit organization we named the Society of Permanent Cosmetic Professionals (SPCP). I am the Director of Education for the International Institute of Permanent Cosmetics in Fountain Valley, California, and also the Clinical Director of Research and Development for Tri-Lab Products. In the past ten years, I have lectured to over 10,000 physicians, dentists, nurses, and beauty professionals. I have performed clinical procedures on movie stars, models, and even NFL football players.

I am the only permanent cosmetic makeup technician appointed to the California Conference of Local Health Officers Task Force. The task force recommends legislation concerning licensing, training, sanitation, and other issues related to tattooing, body piercing, and permanent cosmetics.

I am a member of Who's Who Worldwide and a member of Who's Who Registry for my research in the field of microdermal pigmentation. I have worked with world-renowned burn specialists and plastic and reconstructive surgeons and dermatologists. My greatest joy comes from the confident smiles of clients and patients, particularly burn patients and cancer patients. No amount of money could equal that satisfaction.

I have been a contributing author to numerous trade publications and for the publications *Aesthetic Restoration of the Disfigured Face* by Dr. Elliot Rose (Chapter 8) and *Beautiful Again: Restoring Your Image and Enhancing Body Changes*, by Jan Willis of the Cleveland Clinic. One of my favorite burn patients, Marni, is featured in *Michael Marron's Instant Makeover Magic*.

I have written five educational manuals for various schools in the field of microdermal pigmentation, made numerous presentations on tattooing to state boards of cosmetology, medical conferences, and national trade shows and conventions. In the past year I have appeared on "Special Assignment" on CBS, "The Rise and Shine Show," "Woman's Lifetime Network," and "Extra."

Like all jobs, this one has both rewards and drawbacks. When you own your own business, you put in long hours and get no paid sick days, holidays, or vacation time. There is the occasional client who is dissatisfied, but the pros far outweigh the cons. I can create my own hours, take time off to enjoy my family and friends, and know that I am growing professionally while providing a valuable service to both clients and PCM students.

GETTING IN AND MOVING UP

Most technicians choose to set up their practice in salons where they are currently working. Some may rent rooms from salons, spas, physicians, and dentists. The majority of technicians do not want to be employees. Fees and commissions will vary depending on whether the technician is renting a room or not.

Susan Church advises, "Continuing education is mandatory if you want to be successful in this industry. Read SPCP Newsletters and attend a yearly conference to keep up with the latest technology."

EMPLOYMENT FORECAST

The May 1997 issue of *Forbes* magazine listed permanent cosmetics as one of the top ten fastest-growing businesses and money-makers. As the popularity of the procedure increases, employment of permanent cosmetic technicians is expected to grow much faster than the average for all occupations. Busy career women with increasingly impressive salaries are expected to contribute to the demand for permanent cosmetics. Part of the growth can also be attributed to the interest of dermatologists and surgeons in providing their patients with additional options for improving their appearances. Also, the current tattoo craze for body tattoos is expected to create an increase in corrective pigment camouflage as people with tattoos eventually decide they want them removed.

EARNINGS

The minimum price for a single procedure is about $375. This means that a permanent cosmetic technician who performed only one procedure a week could expect to bring in $18,750 by working 50 weeks of the year. At two procedures a week, the figure jumps to $37,500. Using a medium price per procedure of $525 and two procedures a week, the technician would gross $52,500. One procedure a day at the medium price would bring in $131,250.

While these figures are impressive, technicians have expenses. They *must* be insured because of the possibility of malpractice suits. They have to meet overhead expenses such as rent, utilities, and salaries for support personnel. Equipment, supplies, advertising, and advanced training must be subtracted from the gross figure. Nonetheless, it is easy to see that permanent cosmetics is a lucrative business.

PROFESSIONAL CONNECTIONS

For information about a career as a permanent cosmetic technician and schools offering training, contact

American Association of Cosmetology Schools
15825 N. 71st Street, Suite 100
Scottsdale, AZ 85254
Phone: (800) 831-1086
Web site: *http://www.beautyschools.org*

Society of Permanent Cosmetic Professionals
655 Enterprise Drive, Suite 200
Rohnert Park, CA 94928
Phone: (707) 586-2982
Web site: *http://www.spcp.org*

National Cosmetology Association
401 N. Michigan Avenue
Chicago, IL 60611
Phone: (312) 644-6610
Web site: *http://NCA-now.com*

RESOURCES

BOOKS

Church, Susan. *Permanent Cosmetics A to Z.* Newport Beach, CA: Action Publishing, 1998.

Church, Susan. *Permanent Cosmetics for the Consumer.* Newport Beach, CA: Action Publishing, 1999.

Wright, Crystal A. *The Hair, Makeup and Styling Career Guide.* Los Angeles, CA: Set the Pace Publishing Group, 1997.

MAGAZINES

American Salon
270 Madison Avenue
New York, NY 10016

Les Nouvelles Esthetiques
306 Alcazar Avenue
Coral Gables, FL 33134

WEB SITES

Society of Permanent Cosmetic Professionals:
http://www.spcp.org

A FEW KEY POINTS TO REMEMBER

- Eyeliner, eyebrows, and lip color are the most popular permanent cosmetic services.

- At the present time, PCM is not well regulated in most states. It is essential to investigate any training program very carefully to be sure you will learn enough to perform competently.

- Permanent cosmetic technicians work with surgeons to help burn survivors and cancer patients.

- PCM is one of the fastest-growing and best-paying careers within the cosmetology field.

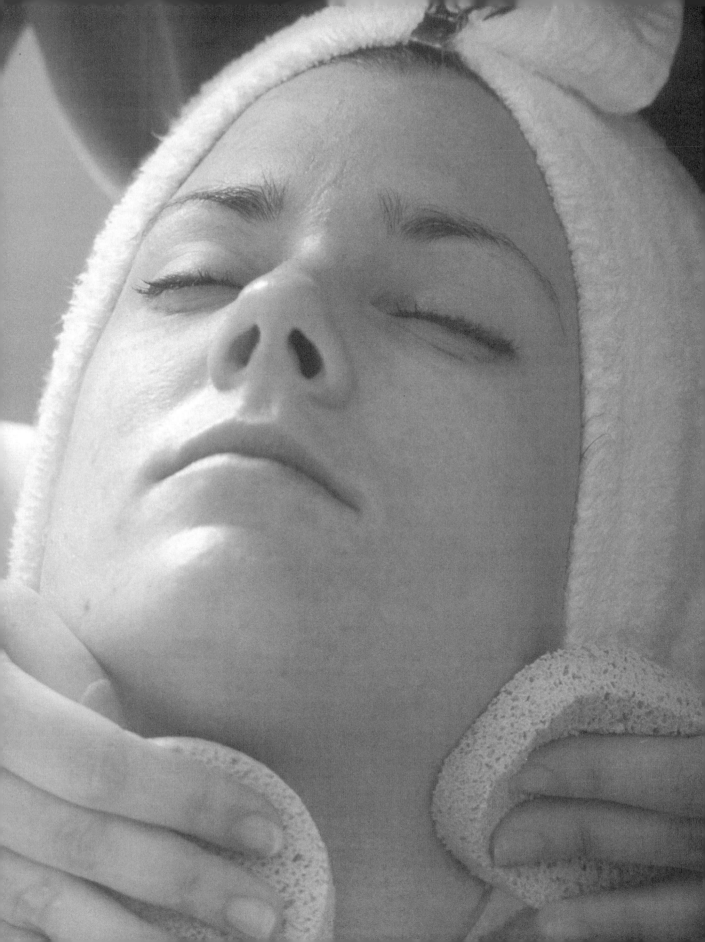

CHAPTER EIGHT

Electrologist

I f you've ever been embarrassed or annoyed by hair in the "wrong" places, you are not alone. Millions of men and women plagued by this problem have turned to electrolysis; a procedure that is medically recognized as the only permanent method of hair removal. Electrologists work in either medically-oriented or cosmetology-oriented settings, helping clients improve their appearance and self-esteem by removing unwanted hair.

Only 32 states require licensing for electrologists, and requirements vary from as few as 120 hours to as many as 1,100. The American Electrology Association inaugurated an internationally recognized certification program in 1986, and passing the IBEC (International Board of Electrologists Certification) examination is a valuable additional credential to licensing. When you have completed electrology training and passed the IBEC exam, you become a Certified Professional Electrologist. The Society of Clinical and Medical Electrologists also has a certification program. Continuing education and recertification are required to maintain the CPE classification.

Licensing

As of January, 1998, electrology licensing was necessary in all of the following states:

Alabama	Michigan
Arkansas	Montana
California	Nebraska
Connecticut	New Hampshire
Delaware	New Jersey
District of Columbia	New Mexico
Florida	Nevada
Hawaii	North Carolina
Idaho	North Dakota
Indiana	Ohio
Iowa	Oklahoma
Kansas	Oregon
Louisiana	Rhode Island
Maine	Tennessee
Maryland	Utah
Massachusetts	Wisconsin

Electrology as a career offers above-average earnings, the personal satisfaction of helping others, the challenge of solving problems, and the opportunity to be an entrepreneur and set your own hours. Students should become familiar with the licensing requirements of their state before they begin to train.

THE RIGHT STUFF

Successful electrologists have outgoing personalities and communicate easily with others. Since electrology clients are often anxious or nervous about the use of needles, it is important to be patient and empathetic. A reassuring and positive working style is helpful. Electrologists often wear lab coats or uniforms to promote a neat and professional appearance. Since many electrologists are in business for themselves, a knowledge of business principles and practices is imperative.

WHAT ELECTROLOGISTS DO

Electrolysis is performed using two basic techniques and/or a combination of the two. Both use electrical current to destroy the hair. After cleansing the skin with antiseptic, the electrologist inserts a very fine sterile probe next to the hair in the hair follicle. Electrical current is distributed through the probe, and the hair is easily lifted out using tweezers. The skin itself is not actually punctured, and the process causes little discomfort.

Most electrology clients are women who want facial hair removed. The most common areas are the chin, above and below the lips, and around the eyebrows, but some women want hair removed from the bikini line, abdomen, breasts, forearms, or underarms. Men come in to have hair removed from the area between the eyebrows, around the outside of the ears, or the shoulders.

WHAT THE JOB IS *REALLY* LIKE

The electrologist tailors the treatment program to each individual patient. Sessions are usually scheduled on a weekly basis, and each one can last from 15 minutes to an hour. Hairs come in on different growth cycles, and the best results are obtained when the hair is in its active growing stage; therefore, a series of electrolysis sessions are scheduled over a period of time.

Tracey Francis, who is profiled below, points out that a lot of time and thought go into advertising, especially when starting a new business. She spends a lot of time cleaning the office and sterilizing equipment. Some of her day is taken up by bookkeeping and accounting. The time that is left is spent either working with customers or waiting for people to call and make appointments.

A Person Who's Done It

MEET TRACEY FRANCIS

VITAL STATISTICS

Tracey Francis, 30, recently opened Finally Free Electrolysis in Clifton Park, New York. The business has already performed better than anyone had predicted. Tracey and her husband, Shawn, who runs the business with her, are excited about the possibilities for the future.

My own electrologist talked me into training for this career. I graduated from Berkowitz School of Electrolysis in August, 1998, and trained with a private practice for over a year after graduation to get more experience. Then we opened Finally Free. I am currently training for my CPE (Certified Professional Electrologist) license. I am a member of several associations, which allows me to talk to industry professionals on a regular basis, and this helps me to keep learning too.

I've found out that this is not a business that lends itself very well to hiring employees because people become very loyal to their electrologist, and it is easy for employees to steal your business from you if they leave. I've also found that it is very expensive to advertise.

Since the business is fairly new, my schedule is still not full. Unfortunately many of my appointments cannot be scheduled consecutively, so I end up waiting around the office for my next appointment. This can be pretty boring and unproductive, so I am making an effort to try to schedule people back to back. For now I put about 20 hours a week into the business. We're working hard to promote brand recognition and sincere loyalty from our customers. So far this seems to be working, and I'm hopeful that the business will continue to grow.

The good thing about being in business for yourself is the flexible schedule. For the most part, I am diligent about not letting the business interfere with my personal life. There is also the reward of helping people feel better about themselves.

I am also proud of how well my husband and I work together. He is very supportive of me and we are learning how to deal with typical personality differences that people in the regular workplace would not be patient enough to work through. I would say that this process is making our marriage even stronger.

The service we offer is pretty straightforward. We don't try to tell clients they need our services. We feel strongly that our purpose is to make clients feel better about themselves, so we pretty much let the client decide which services they want from us. We know what it is like to have an electrologist tell us how badly we "need" an area worked on, when we feel fine just the way we are. We don't ever want to do that to our clients.

My husband chides me about how tight-lipped I am, but I see it as an advantage in this profession. I think it helps to build trust in my clients. They know they can trust me not to gossip about them, and that is important.

As far as the future goes, competition and technology will continue to be the greatest challenges. There is always the possibility that some new break-through will replace electrolysis. People have been trying for a century to solve the problem of unwanted hair, and electrolysis is still the only proven permanent method. But it's a new millenium. You never know what is on the horizon.

GETTING IN AND MOVING UP

Many new electrology licensees begin their careers in established medical clinics or private offices, or in salons where electrolysis is offered. They may work for a time as assistants to experienced electrologists before they begin taking on their own clients. Working in an established practice is a good way to start out because beginners do not have to buy their own equipment. Also, new electrologists must build a clientele, and working in an existing office or salon provides a ready resource of referrals and walk-in clients.

Tracey Francis advises beginning electrologists to go to work for someone located fairly far away from the area where they are thinking of opening their own practice. "This will help your employer feel less threatened by you, and you'll likely get better training from them. When you leave, you can do so on good terms and still have connections, which never hurts."

Advancement as an electrologist comes through gaining experience and building a good reputation. Referrals from physicians add credibility as well as clientele. The American Electrology Association recommends that electrologists remain active learners. The AEA and other professional associations sponsor workshops and other educational events. Belonging to one of the professional organizations helps electrologists keep abreast of what is happening in the field, and is a good way to network with others.

"I would always encourage as much schooling as anyone can get," adds Tracey Francis. "However, I think most electrologists fail because they lack the business knowledge. Taxes and marketing are probably the worst pitfalls."

EMPLOYMENT FORECAST

It is expected that there will be a moderate increase in the number of electrologists needed in the coming decade. More unwanted hair tends to sprout as women and men age, and the aging baby boomers should create a greater need for electrology services. Electrology is more and more being seen as an allied health field rather than a cosmetology field, and referrals by physicians should augment the need for qualified electrologists.

EARNINGS

What an electrologist earns is dependent on many factors. The first is how many clients are seen in a day. A 15-minute treatment can run anywhere from $20 to $30; half an hour averages around $50, while an hour can cost $100 or more. The electrologist often has to split this fee with a clinic or salon, or if self-employed, must pay overhead expenses. Even so, the American Electrology Association estimates that a full-time established electrologist can earn up to $50,000 a year.

PROFESSIONAL CONNECTIONS

American Association of Cosmetology Schools
15825 N. 71st Street, Suite 100
Scottsdale, AZ 85254
Phone: (800) 831-1086
Web site: *http://beautyschools.org*

American Electrology Association (AEA)
106 Oak Ridge Road
Trumbull, CT 06611
Phone: (203) 374-6667
Web site: *http://www.electrology.com*

International Guild of Professional Electrologists
803 N. Main Street
High Point, NC 27262
Phone: (800) 830-3247
Web site: *http://www.igpe.org*

Society of Clinical and Medical Electrologists
132 Great Road, Suite 200
Stow, MA 01775
Phone: (508) 461-0313

RESOURCES

BOOKS

Cotter, Louise and Frances London Dubose (contributor). *The Transition: How to Become a Salon Professional.* Albany, NY: Milady Publishing Corp., 1996.

Hoffman, Lee. *Salon Dialogue: For Successful Results.* Albany, NY: Milady Publishing Corp., 1998.

MAGAZINES

Dermascope
3939 E. Highway 80, Suite 408
Mesquite, TX 75150

Skin, Inc.
362 S. Schmale Road
Carol Stream, IL 60188-2787

WEB SITES

Aesthetics International Association:
http://www.beautyworks.com/aia

Beauty Professionals Network:
http://www.beautytech.com

A FEW KEY POINTS TO REMEMBER

• Electrolysis is the only permanent method for removal of unwanted hair.

• Although electrology is not licensed in all states, an electrologist still needs training and some kind of certification. National certification as a CPE is available through professional organizations.

• Electrology offers above-average earnings, the chance to help others, and the flexibility of being self-employed.

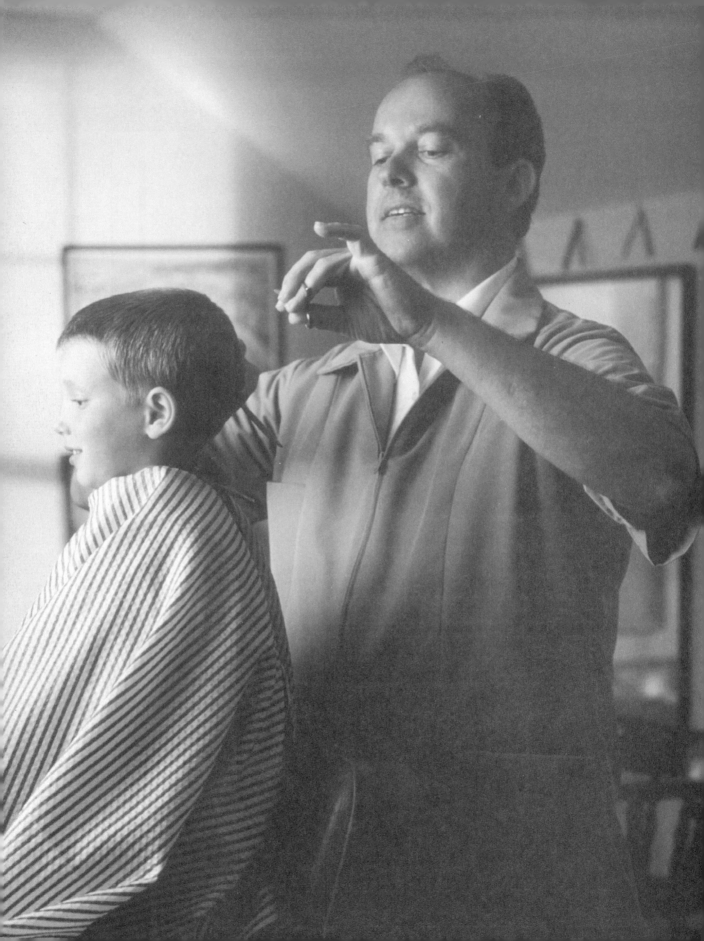

CHAPTER NINE

Barber

I n primitive times, barbers were medicine men and priests—the most important men of their tribes. Until the 1400s, in addition to cutting hair and trimming beards, barbers served as surgeons and dentists. Today, barbers provide a number of services to improve the appearance and condition of their customers' hair.

THE RIGHT STUFF

Barbers must know the art of customer service: assessing needs and providing what the customer wants. It helps to be an active listener and to ask questions to keep the conversation moving. "The corner barbershop" has always been known as a men's social center, and there are still hundreds of shops where the tradition continues.

Barbers need to be able to visualize how a style will look on a customer. This involves consideration of the bone structure of the head and of the facial features. To complete the cut, a barber must have steady hands and good coordination.

Barbers must be licensed in all states. Requirements vary from state to state. Courses may be taken through vocational-technical programs, at community colleges, or at private barbering schools. The courses are similar to the hairdressing component of the cosmetology curriculum, and take six to nine months to complete. In many states barbers have the option of training through apprenticeship programs, which usually last two years. After completion of either an approved barbering course or an apprentice program, prospective barbers take their state board examination. Barbering is still primarily a male occupation, but a small percentage of women do enter it.

WHAT BARBERS DO

Barbers perform the services of cutting, shaping, trimming, coloring, and shampooing hair. Some barbers curl and straighten hair as well. Barbers also have traditionally given shaves and trimmed and shaped beards and mustaches.

Barbers work in many locations: shops in residential neighborhoods, in downtown business districts, in shopping centers, and in airports, resorts, and hotels. Some work in combination barber and beauty shops. Three-fourths of barbers own their own shops. Barbers do most of their work in one small area with their chair as its center. They stand on their feet most of the day, and use their arms and hands continually.

WHAT THE JOB IS *REALLY* LIKE

When a patron arrives at the shop, the first thing the barber asks is what kind of services the person wants. Perhaps the customer wants to let his hair grow a little longer on the top, but wants the sides and back trimmed and shaped. Maybe he wants "a buzz," a "bowl," or a "West Point."

The barber may use clippers, scissors, a comb, a razor, and a blow dryer to style the customer's hair. The barber may also shave the patron's beard and massage the face, neck, and scalp. Finally, the barber may recommend that the customer buy certain supplies available at the shop such as shampoo or styling products.

Seventy-five percent of barbers own their own shops. This means they must take care of business details such as paying the shop's bills, ordering supplies, and keeping financial records. They must also supervise employees. Rather than working less because they have others working for them, they have to work harder.

Jan Harris and Sharon Kizziah-Holmes worked together at a barbershop for six years before deciding to open their own. Experienced in both barbering and cosmetology, they opened a full-service salon in Springfield, Missouri. They named their salon The Barber Shop.

"We chose that name because we know men are leery of going into a "salon," but women will go wherever they get their hair done well. We didn't want to be just the neighborhood barber shop; we wanted to be full service, and it worked," says Sharon.

Three years later, a retiring barber contacted the partners about buying his four-chair shop. "We discussed the options and decided to buy the little shop. The Sunshine Barber Shop had been in business since 1957, and still had the original fixtures. It was a 'men only' kind of atmosphere and we were determined to keep it that way. The first thing we did was change the name to The Barber Shop Too. My husband, Dennis, went to barber school a couple of years ago, and he runs the little shop while Jan and I remain at the salon."

While Sharon works on clients, she is often interrupted to attend to various details of running the business. There are always phone calls, suppliers to talk with, and client and employee concerns to be dealt with.

"Oh, well, that's what you get when you own a business," says Sharon. "And just think, I have it easy because I have a partner and we help each other. Her day is just as hectic, just in different ways."

Two People Who've Done It

MEET JACOB MOORE AND ZEB THOMAS

VITAL STATISTICS

Jake, 20, and Zeb, 21, work together at The Barber Shop in Springfield, Missouri. Both attended the Academy of Hair Design and graduated in 1998.

"I did a little of everything before I became a barber," says Jake. "I worked on roofs in the summer and in grocery stores in the winter. I was even a telemarketer, calling people up to try to sell them long-distance service."

Zeb worked in construction, in restaurants, and in fiberoptics. "Now I'm proud I have a skill in something and a career in it," he says.

"I like knowing I make people look the way they want to look," says Jake. "I listen to what the customers have to say and what they are wanting out of the haircut. Then I cut their hair into what I have pictured."

Facial shapes and personality play a part in haircutting for Zeb, especially when he cuts women's hair. Most of his clients, however, are men. "Men will tell you what they want most of the time," he notes. "If they don't, I make suggestions and see what they say."

Zeb and Jake agree that a good barber needs to be tactful and patient, a good listener, and a bit of a salesman. They believe you can learn the basics of barbering at a good barber school, but that education does not stop at graduation.

"If you didn't do a good job in barber school, then you're probably not going to like being a barber. But I'd say 60 percent of what you learn comes after you get out of school," says Zeb. "After you get out you learn to polish your haircuts. You really have to watch what you do because there is no teacher there to fix things if you do something wrong."

"You have to pay attention to other barbers. They know things you don't," advises Jake. "If you do your job and work hard, things will come to you. Opportunities and money do come your way in this job."

To stay current with what is happening in their business, the two read books and magazines, take classes, and attend shows and other events.

Zeb and Jake arrive at the shop at around 9:00 A.M. There are a few early customers. Then things slow down until around noon, when they get busy and stay that way until around 3:00. There is a brief lull, and then business picks up again at around 5:00.

Both barbers work a 40-hour week, and they like the shop's relaxed atmosphere and their flexible schedules. "If you have to be somewhere, you can get time off," explains Jake.

"I'm starting to get a pretty good clientele. I see about eight to ten people a day for haircuts, color, wax—a little of everything," he adds. "It takes a while to make good money, and you're on your feet all day, but I can live with that."

"Sometimes people are grumpy or business is really slow," adds Zeb, "but all your clients who didn't come in this week will come in the next."

"I know I'm part of a good crew and that feels good," says Jake.

GETTING IN AND MOVING UP

Barber colleges assist their graduates in finding work, and newspaper ads and employment agencies are other sources of job openings. Many barbers belong to unions, the largest being the United Food and Commercial Workers International Union. New graduates may enlist the help of the union in finding work. Barbers usually begin as Licensed Barber Apprentices. After they obtain additional experience, they become Journeyman Barbers or Master Barbers.

Bill Laswell, owner of Laswell's Barber Shop in Indianapolis, Indiana, offers the following advice: "Find a successful barber who is willing to be your mentor. I got lucky and got a job in 1961 working for one of the best barbers in Cincinnati, and he taught me the skills that I still use today."

Barbers advance by developing a list of loyal clientele. They may move to a shop that is in a more prestigious area, or they may open their own shop.

EMPLOYMENT FORECAST

The Bureau of Labor Statistics predicts a 10 percent decline in the number of barbers employed by 2006, but this is an average figure that does not apply to all states. In about half of the states, employment for barbers is expected to increase by the year 2006.

The need for barbering services seems to be directly related to trends in men's styles. Bill Laswell, who has been a barber for 39 years, says he had to change with the times when "some guys named the Beatles" came along and long hair styles came into vogue. He learned to do perms and color. "Everybody was a 'stylist,' and nobody wanted to be a barber, no matter how much money they made." Bill took time away from barbering and worked in real estate and at a car dealership, but in 1991 he decided to go back to the career he loved, and opened Laswell's Barber Shop. "A funny thing had happened during my absence from barbering—the kids started getting haircuts. They liked going to the barber. They couldn't get their hair cut short enough or often enough to suit them. The skills I learned in the sixties were in great demand and there was a shortage of people with those skills. My barbershop was successful beyond my wildest dreams. The kids were back. Dads bring their sons to the shop and sons bring their dads to the shop. It's an important part of male passage."

EARNINGS

Barbers who are not self-employed generally earn either a commission or a set fee for each service performed. Commissions range from 40 percent to 80 percent. Most barbers also receive tips. Earnings depend on the size, type, and location of the shop. Midrange earnings for barbers in the United States are $13,000 to $23,400 annually. These figures, however, apply only to barbers who work for someone else, not to those who own their own shops. It is not unusual for a barber to earn $20 or more an hour after a few years of experience and after a steady client base has been secured. Bill Laswell has this advice: "The most important thing to remember is that skill and speed will enable you to earn a decent living. Being able to do six good haircuts an hour at $11 each will earn you much more than two haircuts an hour at $20 a cut."

PROFESSIONAL CONNECTIONS

Beauty and Barber Supply Institute
11811 N. Tatum Boulevard #1085
Phoenix, AZ 85029-1625
Phone: (800) 468-2274
Web site: *http://www.bbsi.org*

National Association of Barber Boards
77 S. High Street, 16th Floor
Columbus, OH 43266-0304
Phone: (614) 466-5003

Hair International/Associated Master Barbers and Beauticians of America
P.O. Box 273
124-B East Main Street
Palmyra, PA 17078
Phone: (717) 838-0795

RESOURCES

BOOKS

Lamb, Catherine. *Milady's Life Management Skills for Cosmetology, Barber-Styling, and Nail Technology*. Albany, NY: Milady Publishing Corp., 1996.

Wright, Crystal A. *The Hair, Makeup and Styling Career Guide*. Los Angeles, CA: Set the Pace Publishing Group, 1997.

MAGAZINES

American Salon
270 Madison Avenue
New York, NY 10016

Modern Salon
P.O. Box 1414
Lincolnshire, IL 60069

Salon News
P.O. Box 5035
Bentwood, TN 37024-9809

A FEW KEY POINTS TO REMEMBER

- Barbers must know the art of customer service.
- "The corner barbershop" is still known as an unofficial social club for men.
- Barbers' services include cutting, shaping, trimming, coloring, and shampooing hair.
- Many barbers belong to unions, the largest being the United Food and Commercial Workers Union.
- The need for barbering services seems to be directly related to trends in men's styles.
- The physical demands of being a barber include standing on your feet most of the day and using your arms and hands continually.
- Barbers must be licensed in all states.
- Three-fourths of barbers own their own shops.

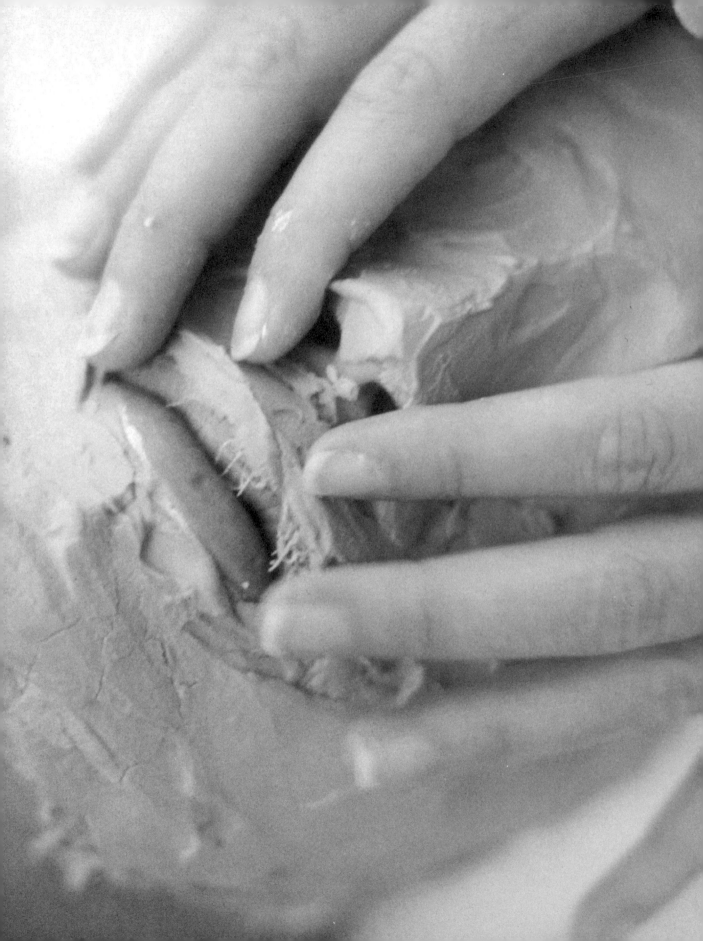

CHAPTER TEN

Day Spa Employee

I f your life has ever seemed so hectic that you felt like shouting "Stop the world! I wanna get off!" you can understand why day spas have become increasingly popular over the past decade. They provide a place to "drop out" for an hour or a day, refresh, and regroup.

In a 1999 *American Spa-Goer Survey* conducted on behalf of the International Spa Association, 7 percent of the people surveyed had attended a day spa at least once during the previous year, and 32 percent said they had an interest in doing so in the future. The primary reason they cited was relaxation. Exercise and fitness were at the bottom of the list.

In addition to cosmetology services such as skin, hair, and nail care, day spas offer a number of treatments that employees learn to administer by observation, hands-on training, taking workshops at trade shows, through classes offered at alternative health institutions, or by correspondence.

THE RIGHT STUFF

Because clients go to day spas to feel relaxed and pampered, day spa employees must present themselves as healthy and positive. The client hopes to enter a slower-paced world at the spa, and the most successful employees have a laid-back way of moving and talking. The spa client's needs are number one, and employees strive to make each client feel it's his or her special day. A sincere enjoyment of caring for others is an essential trait.

WHAT DAY SPA EMPLOYEES DO

Most day spa visitors buy a package of services and treatments, and several employees are involved in taking care of the client. At the Visions Day Spa in Ocean City, Maryland, a client who chooses the "Vision Tranquility" package enjoys a basic European facial, a full-body Swedish massage, a deluxe spa pedicure, a regular manicure, a custom haircut, makeup application, and lunch. The client would work with several different employees during the day.

- Full-body treatments are a hallmark of the day spa. Massage relaxes chronic tension and constricted muscles. Depending on the individual client's needs, treatments such as salt glows, body polishes, and body wraps may be chosen.

- No package would be complete without a cleansing, relaxing facial. Amy Craddock, an esthetician who works at a day spa in Richmond, Virginia, combines Ayurvedic theory with her facial treatments. Ayurveda is a holistic system of healing that evolved in ancient India. It focuses on establishing and maintaining balance of the life energies. "I was fortunate enough to study under Melanie Sachs, a pioneer in bringing Ayurveda to the skin care industry," explains Amy. "In addition to Ayurveda, I am also certified in foot reflexology and La Stone therapy. All of these are related to balancing the body's energies, relaxing, and clarifying the mind. It's the idea that you are beautiful on the outside when you are beautiful on the inside."

- Reflexology is another popular choice of day spa clients. Originally called "Zone Therapy," reflexology is the study of reflexes in the hands and feet, which correspond to all parts of the body. A client might schedule reflexology alone, or enjoy it as a complement to a manicure, pedicure, or full-body massage.

- Hot and cold therapy have long been recognized as beneficial to the body. It has been commonplace for hundreds of years for Scandinavians to rejuvenate by sitting in a hot sauna followed by a plunge into an icy pool of water. La Stone therapy produces alternately sedating and energizing body responses through the use of hot and cold stones. When applied to certain points on the back, the stones are said to produce miraculous results.

- Aromatherapy, said to stimulate the immune system and restore the body and spirit, has been a popular healing method in Europe for decades, and is beginning to gain recognition in the United States. Certified aromatherapists create an individual fragrance blend for each client, depending on his or her needs. Aromatic massage is one of the main aspects of Ayurvedic medicine.

- Cosmetic aromatherapy combines essential oils with facial, skin, body, and hair care products.

- Massage aromatherapy combines massage with essential oils either through direct application to the skin or by diffusing the fragrant oil into the environment.

In addition to these services, many day spas also offer nutritional counseling, yoga sessions, acupressure, water therapies, and even low-intensity aerobics classes. Day spa employees are needed in every area to advise and encourage clients.

WHAT THE JOB IS *REALLY* LIKE

"My day begins at about 7:30 A.M., when I arrive at the spa and look over my schedule for the day," says Amy. "There is quite a bit of preparation work that can be done in advance, so I get everything lined up. My first appointment is at 8:00 A.M., and they run until 12:30 P.M. They could be a combination of anything: half an hour of reflexology, a body wrap, some facials, and occasionally even a set of nails."

"I always take a break at 12:30 P.M. I live close enough to walk home for lunch, and it is good to get away for a little while and refocus my own energy. It's an important part of the job to be friendly, positive, and energetic, and having a midday break is helpful.

"In the afternoon, I have more appointments similar to those in the morning; then in the evening, I teach skin care and nail classes. I work about 45 hours a week, but that is my choice. I pack that all into four days, and then take three days off."

A Person Who's Done It

MEET AMY CRADDOCK

VITAL STATISTICS

When Amy Craddock, 25, signed on as a receptionist at a large day spa, she never dreamed that doing so would eventually take her on an expense-paid trip to Thailand. Here's how it happened.

I was young when I graduated from high school, just 17, and I didn't really know what I wanted to do, but I knew I needed to get a job of some kind. We had just moved to Richmond, Virginia, and my job search turned up a position as a receptionist at a day spa downtown called "Nesbit, the Complete Body Salon." In addition to scheduling appointments, I often worked as a helper, so I observed what the various technicians were doing.

I was pretty happy with my job, but when the spa owner suggested he could use another nail technician and offered to send me to school, I figured why not? I understood that knowing how to do nails would be a skill I could always market, and the potential for increased earnings were an incentive too.

Once I got into the world of beauty, though, I found out that I was fascinated with skin care, and that is what I do now for the most part. Virginia is one of a handful of states where there is no licensure required for estheticians, but I began taking every class I could find and learned as much as I could about skin care. I had always spent a lot of time observing various treatments at the spa, and as I learned more about various therapies, the spa itself became a great learning place for me. I still think of myself as the "education queen," because I never stop learning. I am always going to a class, a conference, or a trade show, and I spend a lot of time reading various magazines.

Our spa is in downtown Richmond, and most of our clients are what you would call "young urban professionals" who work downtown. Most of them are not over 35. They make good money, but they work hard for it and tend to have a lot of stress. Our spa is the perfect place for them to de-stress. They learn about what we offer by reading our brochure or talking to one of our clients. Then they might come in for half an hour of reflexology.

While at the spa, they tell us what kinds of problems they're having and we can recommend additional treatments that might be helpful. We sell packages of treatments that make wonderful gifts, for a friend or for oneself. For example, a package might include a massage, facial, manicure, pedicure, and body wrap, with lunch included.

The company has 72 employees, and we have a good health plan that is very reasonable, along with two weeks' paid vacation and the opportunity to earn extra vacation days by not using sick days. I receive a salary, which is unusual in the beauty business, but I think it is something that is starting to change. When people in a spa or salon all work on commission, there is always a feeling of competing with one another. At our spa, the key word is team-work. We all work together to make the spa a great place, not only to be a client but to be an employee too.

Daily on-the-job rewards come with almost every appointment. There is one client in particular who comes to mind. She had very bad adult-onset acne, and was suffering low self-esteem because of it. I was able to help her clear it up, and my reward was watching her whole personality change from a poor self-image to a confident one.

There have been other big rewards, too. I was the first person on the East Coast to be awarded Spa Certification from the International Dermal Institute. My most incredible reward was a ten-day trip to Thailand for a skin care conference, paid for by the spa. I am only 25, so I feel as though I've done quite a bit for a person my age.

In my free time, I'm working on a pet project of mine. Facials involve extractions, and if a person isn't competent, he or she can cause some serious damage. You really need to know what you're doing. So my project is to get skin care licensed in Virginia. I am busy now circulating petitions to accomplish that. I know licensing will help a lot of people to obtain better treatment, and it will be good for the profession, too.

I cannot say that my job has many drawbacks. People might complain about the way a stylist cuts their hair, but how can they complain about how wonderful they feel after they experience an Ayurvedic facial or a reflexology treatment? They go away looking so much happier than when they came in. That makes me feel good, that I can provide them with that great feeling.

GETTING IN AND MOVING UP

If you do not hold a license in cosmetology, Amy Craddock's advice is to get any kind of job you can at a day spa, even as a receptionist or helper. If you demonstrate that you are dependable as well as interested in everything that goes on at the spa, you will be able to move up. She suggests choosing an area or two in which to specialize, then learn as much as you can through hands-on training and classes.

As a licensed cosmetologist, there are numerous day spa opportunities in hair, skin, and nail care. Through continuing education, cosmetologists can increase the number of services they can provide as a compliment to their regular services (for instance, Ayurvedic facials or reflexology and aromatherapy combined with a pedicure) or learn entirely new treatments such as massage and body wraps.

EMPLOYMENT FORECAST

The number of spa visits increased by 16 percent in 1998, according to a survey conducted for ISPA. Thirty-nine percent of those who visited were first-timers. While spas used to be primarily for women, 25 percent of spa-goers are now men.

In 1989 there were about 30 day spas in the United States, according to Spa Finders, a Manhattan-based spa reservation service. In 1999 the number was estimated at 1,600. As Americans make more money, at the expense of more stress in their lives, the popularity of spas is expected to continue to increase. This will mean an increase in the number of employees needed.

EARNINGS

Since day spas generally have more employees than salons, there is a better chance that an employee will receive a salary, health benefits, and paid vacation and sick leave. Also, since the cost of services is generally higher than in an average salon, even if the employee works on a commission basis, he or she will be splitting a higher amount per service. Earnings are probably in the top quarter of those for all cosmetologists, or $27,000 to $32,000 a year. Much depends on the location, the number of hours worked, and the services provided.

PROFESSIONAL CONNECTIONS

American Reflexology Certification Board
P.O. Box 620607
Littleton, CO 80162
Phone: (303) 933-6921

The Day Spa Association
P.O. Box 5232
West New York, NJ 07093
Phone: (201) 865-2065

National Association for Holistic Aromatherapy
P.O. Box 17622
Boulder, CO 80308
Phone: (888) 275-6242

A FEW KEY POINTS TO REMEMBER

- Spa employees are relaxed, positive-attitude people who genuinely enjoy pampering others.

- A cosmetology license can get you a spa job in hair, nails, or skin. You can learn to perform other spa services on the job and by taking classes.

- Compensation at spas tends to be better than in salons.

Massage In Progress

CHAPTER ELEVEN

Massage Therapist

The first written records of massage therapy date back 400 years to ancient China. Massage was recognized as an important healing art in Europe until the Middle Ages, when religious authorities banned it on the grounds that exposure of the body was immoral. Today, there is a virtual "massage revolution" in progress, and the practice has become more popular than ever before.

While it can't cure serious medical disorders, massage therapy can healing, reduce pain, lower blood pressure, and ease tension and stress. An increasing number of salons are opting to include massage therapy in their service menus, and many beauty professionals see it as a wise addition to their portfolios.

THE RIGHT STUFF

Massage therapists need to be in good physical shape themselves to meet the demands of the job. They must enjoy interacting with people, and should have a nurturing side that helps them derive satisfaction from serving others. Massage therapists are usually interested in health in general, and enjoy learning about and discussing with other professionals the latest ideas on exercise, nutrition, and fitness.

Twenty-five states and the District of Columbia regulate massage therapy, meaning that massage therapists need formal training before they can begin practicing. Depending on the state, the therapist who meets certain requirements may then be called licensed, state certified, or registered. There is also a National Certification Board for Therapeutic Massage and Bodywork. Those who meet the Board's standards and pass the national certification exam have the right to put the initials NCTMB after their names. The American Massage Therapy Association maintains an extensive web site at *http://www.amtamassage.org*, where you can find a listing of the addresses and phone numbers of state agencies that regulate massage as well as information on how to contact the national board. The site also gives prospective students tips on choosing the right school and maintains lists of schools accredited by the Commission on Massage Training Accreditation. (Further contact information is at the end of the chapter.)

Of the states that do regulate massage therapy, an average of 500 hours of instruction at an approved school are required. Even if your state does not require licensing, there may be a city or county ordinance affecting massage therapists. A certificate of graduation from a training program is a credential used in unregulated states. Your certificate will hold more weight if it is from an accredited school. As massage therapy grows in popularity, more states are formulating licensing requirements, so it is wise to get the best education you can right at the beginning.

WHAT MASSAGE THERAPISTS DO

Massage therapists stroke, knead, tap, rub, compress, vibrate, and apply pressure to the muscular structure and soft tissues of the body. They use oils, lotions, powders, and other lubricants. They use their hands primarily, but may also use electric vibrators, ultraviolet and infrared light, and water therapy.

The purpose of massage is to stimulate the muscular, nervous, circulatory, and digestive systems. During and following a massage, *endorphins*—hormones that reduce pain sensations and have a positive effect on emotions—are released. As a result, organs function better and there is an overall feeling of tranquility and balance. Massage reduces tension related to stress, headaches, backaches, and neck pain. It increases blood and lymph circulation and brings oxygen to tissues. It can alleviate such conditions as tendonitis, bursitis, arthritis, and fibromyalgia, and can rehabilitate muscle injuries.

Dozens of specialized massage techniques are in use today. Most therapists use a combination of several techniques to attain the desired results for each client.

- Swedish massage is popular for relaxation and stress reduction.

- Shiatsu, a technique based on Oriental philosophy, concentrates on releasing the body's *chi* (healing energy) by applying pressure to certain points.

- Neuromuscular therapy (often abbreviated NMT) is a deep-tissue massage that works well for clients with chronic pain or muscle tension.

WHAT THE JOB IS *REALLY* LIKE

Ed Pacyna, who operates his own massage therapy practice in upstate New York, says his clients' schedules dictate his schedule. "There really isn't such a thing as an average day," explains Ed. "Some days I might start as early as seven and not finish my last massage until eight that evening. The next day I might have only three massages and be done by noon." On other days, Ed does 15-minute chair massages for employees at several local businesses—a newspaper, an attorney's office, and a restaurant.

Since Ed is in business for himself, he spends some time each day on paperwork, insurance claims, and thinking up and implementing new ways to market and promote his practice. Massage therapy, like any business, has its ups and downs. In the resort area where Ed lives, July and August are the busiest.

Ed uses his own experience, input from the client, a combination of techniques, and intuition to tailor the session to each client's needs. "Those needs can change from session to session, too. It depends on what kind of problems they are experiencing when they come in. Ninety percent of the work I do is related to relief from specific problems. Very few people come in just because they want to relax."

Massage therapists learn quickly how important it is to take care of themselves. "It can be emotionally as well as physically draining. I try not to schedule more than two or three back-to-back appointments," says Ed. "You have to give your arms a rest or you'll burn out."

A Person Who's Done It

MEET ED PACYNA

VITAL STATISTICS

For eight years, Ed Pacyna, 34, worked in an auto body shop. Then he "switched to human bodies." Ed still enjoys restoring old cars as a hobby, but he has found greater rewards in restoring pain-free mobility to his massage therapy clients.

I played football in high school all four years, but in my senior year I tore up my thigh pretty badly. After graduation, I went to school to learn auto body repair and found a job. I worked my way up to body shop manager, which meant I had a lot more interaction with the customers than I had had in the past. I realized how much I really enjoyed that part of the job.

The chemicals used in the body shop were beginning to get to me, and that old football injury was giving me problems as well. I could feel it in my leg and back, and I was finding it harder to do the crouching and bending that are part of the job. The mother of a girl I was seeing at the time convinced me to try massage therapy. I was sold on it almost from the first session. After about three months of weekly sessions, I realized I had no more pain. I continued the massage sessions for about a year and a half, and by that time I was going to massage school myself.

It happened that my girlfriend's mom had been trying to convince her sister to go to massage therapy school, and she had all the literature about the career and where to get training. As it turned out, I was the one who ended up going to school. It required quite a commitment and a lot of determination because I had to drive 3-1/2 hours one way to school, stay there and attend classes for three days, then drive back home and work at the body shop. I knew massage therapy was for me, though, and I knew I would finish the program and do well.

When I got my license, I went to work at Sagamore, a resort on Lake George. It was a great way to get a lot of experience working on different kinds of people with all diffferent kinds of problems. Since there were new clientele each week, I saw every kind of muscle problem imaginable, and got to use a lot of various techniques.

I had already bought a house in Queensbury before I ever started going to massage therapy school, so it seemed logical for me to open my own practice in my home soon after I became licensed. I have it set up so that the massage room is separate from the rest of the house. There is a separate entrance and restroom facilities; it's all very professional.

A massage therapist has to be a nurturing, down-to-earth person who really takes pleasure in helping others. I've had people say things like, "Wow, if you did eight or ten massages a day you could really make some big bucks." However, your motivation for getting into this profession just can't be because of the money. In the first place, there is no way you could do all those massages every day without hurting your arms. But the main thing is, your heart has to be in it. Your rewards have to come from your clients.

I come from a close, loving family, and my parents have always been very supportive of me. Even so, my dad was a little mystified when I told him I was going to become a massage therapist. Then I gave him his first massage, and he understood completely. He said, "God bless you for wanting to help people." Needless to say, I felt pretty great about that.

When a client who has fibromyalgia came to see me for the first time, she was nervous and frightened. She had tried massage before and had found it very painful. Added to that was the emotional burden a lot of doctors put on people with fibromyalgia when they tell them it's all in their heads. They *know* they are hurting all over, all the time. I was very careful and gentle, and yet my client began to cry. I felt terrible, worried I had done something wrong. It turned out she was crying because of the great relief from pain she felt. No amount of money could be worth as much as alleviating another person's misery.

I would like to add another therapist to my practice, possibly a female. I have even thought about opening a spa. I am really glad I got into massage therapy. I plan to continue doing this indefinitely.

GETTING IN AND MOVING UP

As a massage therapist, you may own your own business, work as an independent contractor, or work as an employee. As a self-employed massage therapist, like Ed Pacyna, you probably have a private office or clinic where clients come for massages. You give massages yourself, and possibly you have one or more massage therapists working for you. You do all the advertising, pay all the bills, pay business setup charges, and purchase supplies. Some massage therapists go to their clients' homes; others provide "chair massages" at shopping malls or airports.

Independent contractors provide services through other businesses. For example, you might work at a chiropractor's office or physical therapy clinic, at a day spa, or at a hospital, or you might work through more than one business.

As an employee, you might be a member of the staff at a beauty salon, health club, resort, country club, or medical clinic. As an employee, you will have a better chance of getting insurance benefits, your employer will pay for advertising, and you will be given clients to work on rather than having to find them for yourself. The camaraderie of other massage therapists can be important when you are starting out, too.

Ed Pacyna is certified by the National Certification Board of Therapeutic Massage and Bodywork, is a member of the American Massage Therapy Association, and is a licensed massage therapist in the state of New York. In order to maintain his national certification, he must take 50 hours of continuing education every four years. Continuing education is essential for staying on top of trends.

In many careers, one begins in an entry-level position and then gets promoted to better positions. In massage therapy, you keep the same job title but advance by gaining a reputation that allows you to gradually increase your fees.

EMPLOYMENT FORECAST

According to AMBP figures, more than 900 massage schools graduate over 20,000 students each year. The American Massage Therapy Association's membership tripled during the 1990s. Where will all of these graduates find work? A number of factors contribute to the growing demand.

The profession is becoming more widely recognized by those in the various health care fields: chiropractors, M.D.s, physical therapists, and nurses all recognize the value of massage. Consequently, a growing number of health insurance companies are beginning to cover the costs of massage therapy when recommended by a physician as part of treatment. In a 1995 survey of primary care physicians, 54 percent said they would recommend massage therapy as a complement to their medical treatment.

Alternative Medicine

Alternative medicine is now a $13 billion market, and massage therapy is the form of alternative medicine people say they would be most likely to try first. In 1997, 42 percent of adults in America used some form of alternative care.

The public interest in health, fitness, and well-being has increased dramatically over the past few decades. The corresponding growth of health clubs, gyms, and wellness centers has resulted in a heightened demand for massage therapists. Along the same line, sports teams hire massage therapists to travel with the team and help athletes recover from sore muscles and injuries. Another growth arena for massage therapists is the day spa. As this industry expands and grows, so does the need for massage therapists.

EARNINGS

According to ABMP figures, full-time massage therapists can earn between $40,000 and $60,000 per year. The association points out that since a large number of therapists work less than 20 hours per week, the median income figure for the profession is just under $20,000. Hourly rates range anywhere from $25 to $75, depending on location and the experience and reputation of the massage therapist. Earnings also depend on the physical stamina of the therapist. For example, if he or she is able to give six massages a day at $50 each, gross pay for one day is $300. Another earnings factor is whether the therapist is self-employed or splitting the fee with a salon or other business.

PROFESSIONAL CONNECTIONS

Associated Bodywork and Massage Professionals
28677 Buffalo Park Road
Evergreen, CO 80439-7347
Phone: (800) 458-2267
Web site: *http://www.abmp.com*

American Massage Therapy Association
820 Davis, Suite 100
Evanston, IL 60201-4444
Phone: (708) 864-0123
Web site: *http://www.amtamassage.org*

A FEW KEY POINTS TO REMEMBER

• Even if your state does not regulate massage therapy, you should get the best training you can. You will give your clients better service, and that in turn will help your business to grow.

• Massage therapists work at resorts and spas, health clubs, and salons, in their own offices, in physicians' offices, and at clients' locations.

• The demand for massage therapy is growing rapidly as more and more people become interested in alternative forms of health care.

CHAPTER TWELVE

Manufacturer's Education Representative

I f you are interested in the beauty industry, you probably already know that hundreds of companies manufacture cosmetics of every kind to improve and enhance every inch of us from head to toe. Manufacturers spend millions every year developing new products that make use of recent scientific discoveries, unique ingredients, or other improvements that promise better-than-ever results. These companies are always looking for people who can help them demonstrate their products and increase their sales.

THE RIGHT STUFF

A cosmetology license can be your first step toward working for a beauty supply manufacturer. Dee Manieri is a Greensboro, North Carolina, nail technician who is also educational coordinator and state school coordinator for OPI, a leading manufacturer of professional nail products. Dee points out a number of qualities that are essential for the successful education representative.

First, the rep must be willing to work on weekends and days off in order to attend trade shows. Educators must keep in mind that they are taking part in the training of up-and-coming cosmetologists—for instance, on visits to schools—or educating established salon professionals about how to use the latest products. Educators must know how to manage their time wisely, and must be outgoing and friendly, knowledgeable about the products, professional, sales-oriented, and prompt with paperwork.

Millie Haynam, Midwest Regional Education and Sales Manager for Nail-Tek, emphasizes that a successful education representative must love the work. "Experience is relative," says Millie. "It isn't always about years of experience; it is about the passion behind you." She looks for representatives with professional integrity, a positive attitude, and good communication skills.

WHAT MANUFACTURER'S EDUCATION REPRESENTATIVES DO

There are several different types of education representatives. Most of the educators seen at trade shows also work in salons. They work part time as independent contractors for the manufacturer, sharing their expertise with others.

Some companies hold classes year-round, at salons or through distributors, and educators are needed to teach these classes. There are also educators who work full time for manufacturers, teaching classes at salons and working at shows.

Dee Manieri teaches workshops through beauty supply distributors and also teaches at beauty schools and community colleges in her area. She attends distributor sales meetings, presenting information on new products to their sales staffs. In order to keep up with the material she is teaching others, she must also attend training workshops herself.

When Millie Haynam is not attending a trade show, she might be found writing articles for the company newsletter, researching materials for classrooms, returning phone calls from educators with questions, writing classroom scripts, or working on a special project like a holiday marketing plan.

WHAT THE JOB IS *REALLY* LIKE

A typical weekend at a trade show goes like this for Dee Manieri:

"On Friday I drive to the hotel or convention center where I am staying and check in. The next morning we start setting up the booth. There are usually six educators working the booth, so if we start setting up by 9:00 A.M. we're done by 1:00 or 2:00 P.M. The distributor usually sends two pallets of merchandise they want us to display and sell at the booth. After unpacking everything and taking inventory, we set up the displays. Everything must be priced, and we have to make sure we have clipboards, pens, calculators, a tax chart, invoice forms, and a cash box. It is hard work, and we really need a rest when we're done.

"We also are often asked to attend sales meetings that morning. We go over the products we will be selling for them and meet all the other sales-people associated with the distributor. At another meeting, usually later on in the day, we go over the correct procedure for writing up sales invoices. Some customers pay cash and take the products with them, others put it on an existing sales account, others want the items shipped to them, and so forth. There are often special show discounts, and these are also announced at the meeting.

"Attire for setup day is jeans, tennis shoes, a company T-shirt, and a name tag. On the following day I dress up a bit: dressy black slacks, black dress shoes, an OPI T-shirt or denim shirt, and a big smile! Some distributors will have scheduled classes about products for me to teach, and their customers can attend. The classes are held in a separate room with a classroom-type setting. I arrive in the room with my tote bag stocked with products and demonstrate them to the attendees.

"We also demonstrate products at the booth. The classes and demos are divided up between the group of educators, but we are all very busy with our classes, demos, and selling. We work from 8:30 A.M. to 5:30 P.M. with only half an hour for a quick lunch. Monday is very much like Sunday, except that the booth closes at 3:00 P.M. We then count the inventory we have left at the booth to determine our total sales. (We hope to sell a lot so we will have less to count.) We usually finish up about 5:00 P.M., and then pack what is left into boxes that must be taped up, addressed, and put on pallets. Every show is hard work, but they are rewarding. I always learn something new and meet new people. It is fun to work as part of a team.

"I receive a salary for my work, plus commissions on sales. No taxes are taken out of my pay, so I have to compensate for that. I also work as a nail technician in a full-service salon Wednesday through Friday. Most of my work for OPI is done on Mondays, Tuesdays, and weekends."

Some manufacturer's representatives are involved more with selling and less with education. Their primary job is to call on salons and beauty schools within a given territory and take orders for products. Manufacturer's are always developing new products. So even though these representative positions are more sales-oriented than education-oriented, this type of manufacturer's representative still needs to have a basic understanding of hair, skin, and nail care in order to explain how products work and why their particular products should be chosen over those of the competitors.

A Person
Who's Done It

MEET DEE MANIERI

VITAL STATISTICS

When Dee Manieri, 44, went to beauty school in 1975, she was the only student taking the manicuring course. The "nails explosion" was still a few years away. By the time it came, Dee was ahead of the game and ready to help others learn from her experience.

I got started in the nail industry in 1975. I had been out of high school for only two years and was stuck in a clerical career that was going nowhere. A friend of mine, a manicurist at a local salon, was getting married and moving away. She talked me into taking over her clients. So...I went to beauty school in the mornings and worked in the salon with my friend training me. When I took over her clients, I was one of the few manicurists in town.

In school, I had learned only how to do a basic manicure and pedicure and paper mending wraps. Everything else—sculptured nails, tips, gel, wraps—I learned from attending workshops through beauty supply distributors.

Over the years I worked in many different salons, under different circumstances (commission, salary, or booth rental). I attended many workshops and classes and worked part time as an educator for several nail manufacturers.

I got my present job—educational coordinator and state school coordinator for OPI—by attending an OPI two-day workshop provided through a local beauty supply dealer. The educator who taught the workshop gave me a great reference to OPI. I traveled to Atlanta for four intense days of training where I learned about every product the company manufactures. I had to perform "hands on" on three artificial nail products, take a 100-question written test, and give a 15-minute presentation on one of the company's retail products. The other companies I had worked for had not provided this kind of training, and I found OPI to be extremely professional.

In addition to representing the company at weekend trade shows, I teach workshops on weekdays at schools that have purchased OPI products and do demonstrations at schools that are potential accounts. Workshops last four hours; demos last two hours. I also talk with students and instructors about OPI products they might find beneficial. I show them kits and help them with their orders.

I was very nervous when I taught my first class with a distributor. I had 12 students, and I was so surprised when each of them purchased $100 or more in OPI products. I received commission on those sales, plus my salary for the class!

In addition to the opportunity to make money, it's always nice when I see "Excellent" on the evaluation forms I've passed out after teaching a class, or when a student, instructor, or distributor sends me a letter of appreciation. I save them and paste them in my sales manual. The only real drawback of this job is that there is a lot of travel. It doesn't bother me because I am single and have no children, but it could be a problem for a woman or man with a family.

My goal is to work full time for a nail manufacturer as a district manager or regional manager in my area. I feel that I'm on my way now.

GETTING IN AND MOVING UP

Dee has these suggestions for those who want to get out of the salon and move into work with a manufacturer:

"Attend as many workshops as you can, and get to know the educators teaching the workshops. Attend beauty shows and get to know the people working the booths. Order your products from several reliable distributors in your area, and get to know your sales representatives. Exchange business cards with everyone. Networking really helps, and you never know who may be able to help you find the job of your dreams."

Millie Haynam points out that some manufacturers advertise at their local distributors when they are looking for educators, and some advertise in professional trade magazines and on various web sites. (One good source we found was the BBSI web site at *http://www.bbsi.org*.)

Millie recommends reading sales books, marketing books, and trade publications. She also advises a technique she calls "strengthening the chain." "Focus on a few basic skills you need work on, check them off your list, and move on. Pick your weakest link and work on it, the next weakest, and so on. If you need to polish your speaking skills, enroll in Toastmasters. You also need to mentor someone below you to take your position so you can move up."

She stresses that there are many, many jobs available with manufacturers. Combining your experience and expertise in cosmetology with another of your major strengths can lead you to the right job. Some of the possibilities are artistic director, national or regional sales manager, research and development, design, advertising, and platform artist.

EMPLOYMENT FORECAST

The cosmetology industry as a whole is growing rapidly. Its growth is likely to produce similar expansion in the number of products available and the number of representatives needed to educate salon professionals, and to sell and market products.

EARNINGS

Earnings for educators are largely dependent on the number of trade shows and workshops in which they participate, how well these are attended, and how many products are sold. Full-time representatives can make anywhere from $35,000 to $75,000 plus commission. Educators who work as independent contractors can expect to have their travel, hotel, and meals paid, and some receive a salary for each day spent working for the company. Arrangements can differ dramatically from company to company, so before accepting a job, you should be sure you understand the compensation structure and that you will be able to live with it.

PROFESSIONAL CONNECTIONS

Beauty and Barber Supply Institute
11811 N. Tatum Boulevard #1085
Phoenix, AZ 85028-1625
Phone: (800) 468-2274
Web site: *http://www.bbsi.org*

Cosmetology Advancement Foundation
208 E. 51st Street
New York, NY 10022
Phone: (212) 388-2772

Nail Manufacturers Council
401 N. Michigan Avenue
Chicago, IL 60611
Phone: (312) 245-1595
Web site: *http://www.americanbeauty.org*

A FEW KEY POINTS TO REMEMBER

• Manufacturers' representatives help the companies they work for by demonstrating their products and increasing their sales.

• It is possible to work either part time or full time for a manufacturer.

• A large part of an educator's job is attending trade shows. Another duty is to give workshops and seminars at beauty schools.

• Earnings for manufacturers' reps vary widely and are dependent on many factors.

CHAPTER THIRTEEN

Cosmetology Instructor

There is a growing need for cosmetology instructors to train tomorrow's salon professionals. Performing salon services on clients is quite a bit different from teaching others how to do it. It takes special skills to be a good instructor.

THE RIGHT STUFF

Cosmetology instructors must be knowledgeable about their subject, but teaching requires much more than subject knowledge. Essential skills include the ability to communicate with a diverse group of students, the desire to motivate and inspire students, and the teaching skills needed to respond to the different ways in which students learn. In addition, cosmetology instructors should be organized, dependable, patient, creative, and able to work well with other members of the school staff.

"You can't show favoritism. You have to stay in control emotionally, and you have to criticize in a constructive way that will help students," says Mary

Scott-Rom, 54, who has been teaching cosmetology for 15 years at Kirtland Community College in Roscommon, Michigan. "You have to be willing to do paperwork efficiently. Also, you might have the need for first aid from time to time. You just have to be prepared for anything."

WHAT COSMETOLOGY INSTRUCTORS DO

Cosmetology instructors prepare and present the theoretical and practical fundamentals of cosmetology to students. They prepare lesson plans and teaching units much as teachers of traditional public school courses do, always with their students in mind. If students are having a difficult time with a particular concept, the instructor must create a new technique to help them learn.

Cosmetology instructors may lecture, demonstrate, use films and overhead projectors, use computers, and invite guest speakers and volunteer cosmetologists to the classroom.

They often work one-on-one with students during the practical segments of instruction. Representatives from cosmetic companies may visit and provide workshops for the students. All of these activities must be coordinated by the cosmetology instructor.

Like traditional schoolteachers, cosmetology instructors must develop, administer, and grade tests. They observe and evaluate students as they learn to perform the various cosmetology services, and provide assistance in the areas where students need help. They meet with administrators and other staff and offer ideas for improving the cosmetology program.

Licensing requirements for cosmetology instructors vary from state to state, but a prerequisite in every state is to obtain a cosmetology license. A certain amount of salon experience may also be required.

Instructors' programs vary greatly in the number of hours required, with the average being about 500 hours. Areas of study include orientation to teaching, teaching materials, course outlining and development, lesson planning, presentation techniques, evaluation of students, cosmetology law, and practice teaching in both theory and practical areas.

WHAT THE JOB IS *REALLY* LIKE

"Being an instructor is similar to being a teacher," explains Mary Scott-Rom. "We have lesson plans, time management, attendance records, grades, and so forth. But we also have more paperwork—progress reports for financial aid, and monthly reports required by the state on each student.

"My day at school starts at 7:30 A.M. This gives me time to prepare for the day. At 8:30 we take attendance. Then we go to theory for an hour, which is book work. After that, we start a practical application. Let's say it's a demonstration on haircutting. First I show the students how to hold their combs and scissors, then they have to practice doing it correctly. Next I demonstrate how to section the hair properly. The students have to practice until they have it at least 75 percent correct. We go through the demonstrations and practice on all the steps of the haircutting procedure. It may take a full day just to do the basic procedure.

"I follow my lesson plan, taking time to do the demo step and then giving the students time to practice the same. During one day of school, we give our students seven hours of work. At the end of the day, we help them fill out their "weeklies," which are turned in at the end of the week and are put on state-required monthly reports.

"The students are finished at 4:00 P.M., but I still have more to do. I have office hours for half an hour to an hour. Then when I go home in the evening I plan my next day's lessons, correct and grade tests, make up new tests, or do reports on my computer."

Jackie McGinnis, an instructor at the Pennsylvania Academy of Cosmetology Arts and Sciences, says the most challenging part of teaching is trying to reach all of the students in the classroom. "You constantly have to change your teaching technique so the whole class understands the lesson." Mary Scott-Rom adds, "The most satisfying is when a student is struggling and all of a sudden a little light goes off in them; they get it, they understand, and you are the one who helped them understand. Seeing students come back after they graduate, seeing that they love what they do, and having them credit my teaching to their success—that is very gratifying."

A Person Who's Done It

MEET MARY SCOTT-ROM

VITAL STATISTICS

Like the other cosmetology instructors at Kirtland Community College, Mary Scott-Rom enjoys working as part of a team for the betterment of the students.

The real reason I became an instructor is that a new school was opening in the town where I live, and they needed a "Full Instructor." With my years of experience and with Kirtland Community College's Instructor's Program, I became a licensed instructor and worked there for about two years. I then opened a large salon and substituted at K.C.C. for a year. I have worked at K.C.C. part time (26 hours a week) for 15 years now. I sold my shop six years ago.

The other instructors in the cosmetology program here all love teaching and keeping the students up to date. Most people who become instructors want to grow and advance in their profession and become better people through helping students. Our curriculum is state board-oriented as well as salon-ready. We have all the newest and most up-to-date equipment to work with, including the latest educational videos. Students can borrow videos and books from the "Cos Library." We also have a computer for the students, which we use for client records such as perm, color, and other information about the clients.

I don't think learning has to be boring. I expect my students to read their chapters ahead of time. Since I'm a second-year instructor, these students have already been through the book once. I like to have fun with my students as we learn. Sometimes during theory we play "Jeopardy!" and dart games, and even Bingo. Of course, I also still use the blackboard and overhead projector, and I do demonstrations.

No matter what job you have, I think you get out of it what you put into it. I worked many years before I was offered health, dental, and vision benefits. But there are other rewards, such as when a student's "light bulb" goes on and you know they finally understand something they have been struggling with. Smiling faces and perfect attendance records make me happy, as do students who are doing the best they can even if it isn't completely right.

I really am proud of all of my students, because a lot of them are women who have outside lives away from school. Some are divorced and are looking for a career that will pay them well. Some are single parents who have other jobs and want to better themselves. Most students have at least one job while they are going to school.

One student stands out in my mind as a real overnight success story. She started our program while still in high school. She was dual-enrolled, that is, she went to high school two days a week and to K.C.C. three days a week. She finished the program here not long after she graduated from high school. At the first two salons where she worked, she had bad experiences, and she would call me and cry on my shoulder. She wanted to broaden her horizons. I always told her to set some short-term and long-term goals...and then go for them. In about three years' time she has moved downstate and is a manager of a salon as well as a color technician and a stage demonstrator. She is making well over $2,000 a week take-home pay. And her family thought she'd never make any money in this business!

I have worked in a private school and a public school. I have taught high schoolers and college students. My youngest student was 13 and my oldest was 65. I've taught all kinds of people. I have learned a lot and enjoyed every minute of my 17 years as an instructor—and I'm still going!

GETTING IN AND MOVING UP

The first step is to obtain your instructor's license. Your state cosmetology board can give you information, or you can check requirements with a community college or private beauty college that offers instructor training.

Once you have your license, there are several places to check regularly for job openings. You should be able to do at least part of your checking on-line, as most community colleges and public school systems now post job openings on their web sites.

You may even be able to download an application. This may also be a good way to compare salary and benefit information. Call or visit private beauty schools to find out when and where they post openings.

Even if there are no openings posted at any of the schools where you check, be sure to send your résumé along with a cover letter and completed application form. Schools tend to keep applications on file, and you may get a phone call about a possible job before you even realize there is one available.

Let your cosmetology school know you are interested in teaching. "When we have job openings for instructors, we do advertise in the newspaper," says Rose Charney, a supervisor at Pennsylvania Academy of Cosmetology Arts and Sciences. "We try to hire our own graduates because we know how they were trained and they know our programs."

Mary Scott-Rom recommends getting an Associate's Degree in Cosmetology if you want to make the best money as an instructor. A degree can open doors to other positions in cosmetology education as well.

You can move up to department head, work on curriculum development at a state level, become the admissions director at a private beauty college, help students with financial aid concerns, or even open your own beauty school.

EMPLOYMENT FORECAST

The word is out that cosmetology is a fast-growing career field and that it pays well for a relatively short time spent in training. As more men and women choose to enter the field, more instructors will be needed to teach them. Many cosmetology instructors work part time in teaching and still maintain their businesses as stylists, estheticians, or nail technicians. In addition, a cosmetologist with an instructor's license may have a better chance of being hired as a salon manager or product educator.

EARNINGS

Metro Tech Beauty Academy in Oklahoma City reports earnings for cosmetology instructors at between $12,480 and $35,000 a year, depending on the instructor's experience and the type of school in which he or she teaches. Earnings are also dependent on how many hours an instructor teaches. Community colleges may offer only part-time jobs with no benefits, while a teaching position at a vocational-technical school or public high school is more likely to be full time and to include benefits. Private beauty schools vary greatly in the salaries and benefit programs they offer.

PROFESSIONAL CONNECTIONS

Association for Career and Technical Education
1410 King Street
Alexandria, VA 22314
Phone: (800) 826-9972
Web site: *acte@acteonline.org*

Vocational-Industrial Clubs of America
P.O. Box 3000
Leesburg, VA 20177-0300
Phone (703) 777-8810

RESOURCES

BOOKS

Hoffman, Lee. *Salon Dialogue: For Successful Results*. Albany, NY: Milady Publishing Corp., 1998.

MAGAZINES

1st Hold
4237 Los Nietos Drive
Los Angeles, CA 90027-2911

Les Nouvelles Esthetiques
306 Alcazar Avenue, Suite 204
Coral Gables, FL 33134

Salon News
P.O. Box 5035
Bentwood, TN 37024-9809

WEB SITES

American Salon:
http://hairnet.com

Beauty Professionals Network:
http://www.beautytech.com

A FEW KEY POINTS TO REMEMBER

• Cosmetology instructors must be knowledgeable about their subjects, but additional skills are needed for teaching effectively.

• Like traditional schoolteachers, cosmetology instructors prepare and present lessons, test and evaluate students, and file reports.

• Cosmetology instructors are employed by vocational-technical schools, community colleges, and private beauty colleges.

CHAPTER FOURTEEN

I Graduated! Now What?

The goal of every reputable cosmetology program is to prepare its students to pass the state licensing examination. All states require examination and licensing of cosmetologists and barbers. Most require that nail techs and estheticians be licensed.

Like licensing requirements, the cosmetology examinations themselves vary from state to state. Most states require a practical exam for cosmetology; that is, one where you actually work on a model's hair, do a manicure, and perform a facial in front of examination officials. Some states are moving toward eliminating this portion of the exam as a money-saving measure. They take the school's word for it that you have learned to perform basic cosmetology services, and require only that you pass a written examination.

137

> ### NIC Exam
>
> More than 40 states use a written exam developed by the National-Interstate Council of State Boards of Cosmetology, Inc. (NIC). It is based on the core curriculum of cosmetology courses offered throughout the country. There are 100 multiple-choice questions in areas such as basic principles and concepts, safety and sanitation, physical and chemical services, and hair design. You can take a sample five-question NIC quiz free on-line at *http://www.learnx.com*; the fee for the complete 100-question practice test is $20.

Your instructors will be able to tell you how to apply to take the test, how much the fees will be, and what to expect on the day of the test. Don't forget essential things like your photo I.D. and admission ticket. Be sure to get plenty of sleep the night before the exam. Remember, you have spent the better part of a year preparing for the test. The chances are you will do well.

In some states, you are notified on the spot whether or not you passed the test. In others, you will have to wait several weeks to be notified by mail. Then you can apply for your license and start job hunting!

RÉSUMÉS

WHY WRITE A RÉSUMÉ?

Think of yourself as a product you want to sell. A résumé is like an advertisement for yourself. It tells prospective employers all about you—your strengths, your accomplishments and skills, and your previous job experience. It also tells employers you are serious about your career and that you consider yourself a professional.

You might think your previous job experience is irrelevant unless it was in the cosmetology field, but this is not true. *Any* previous job you've held has some "transferable skills," that is, skills you developed there that will also be helpful in your job as a cosmetologist.

Let's say you have been working part time as a food server:

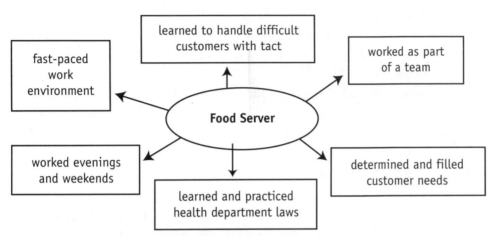

fast-paced work environment

learned to handle difficult customers with tact

worked as part of a team

Food Server

worked evenings and weekends

learned and practiced health department laws

determined and filled customer needs

All of these skills transfer to a job as a cosmetologist, and we haven't even mentioned that you exhibited responsibility by arriving on time for work, by being neat and polite, and by getting along well with others, all traits that might be mentioned in a reference letter or phone call from your previous supervisor.

You can use the worksheet below to create a similar diagram of transferable skills for your previous jobs. Fill out a diagram for each job you've held. When you write your résumé, you can use them for reference.

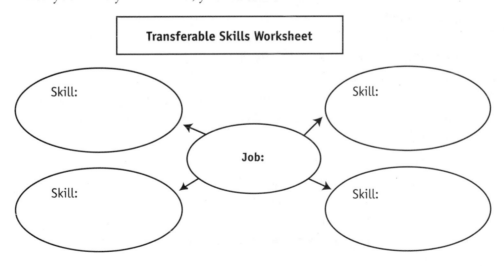

Transferable Skills Worksheet

Skill:

Skill:

Job:

Skill:

Skill:

Remember that any job where you worked with the public gave you customer service experience, even if you merely took orders at a fast-food restaurant. Even baby-sitting requires the person to be responsible, resourceful, patient, and good with children. (You will, after all, be cutting children's hair as well as adults'.)

If you worked in retail sales, a salon owner might see your potential to boost sales of salon products. Or perhaps you were famous for the artistic displays or clever ads you created for the store.

WRITING YOUR RÉSUMÉ

On page 144 you will find a sample résumé for a hairstylist. Notice that after her name, address, and phone number, the job seeker listed her Job Objective. A Job Objective is a very brief description of the job you are hoping to find. You should avoid saying that you will take any job in a salon. Decide exactly what it is you want to do and state that as your Objective. If you really want to style hair, your Objective should say so. At the interview, if you learn that the salon desperately needs someone to do facials one day a week, you can decide then if you are willing to do that and even use it as a bargaining tool; for example, "I'd be willing to do that if you'll pick up the cost of some additional classes in esthetics I feel I need." If you start out by saying you'll take any job, you lose your bargaining power.

Our hypothetical hairstylist summarizes her qualifications next. On the first line, she explains that she is trained and licensed in cosmetology. The other lines highlight personal traits and skills that make her well suited for the job.

In the education section, our job seeker lists her beauty school education first, with a few key points emphasized: her experience in the school salon, her high test scores, and her successful completion of the examination for licensing.

In the work experience section, do not list any jobs you had for only a short while or those that did not work out well (if you were fired or you hated the job, for instance). Instead, concentrate on the transferable skills you discovered. Tell what you liked about the jobs, not what you *didn't* like. Employers hire people with positive attitudes and enthusiasm, not grumblers and whiners.

If you have no previous job experience, you will need to emphasize your education and your extracurricular activities such as volunteer work or hobbies. Maybe you did the makeup for the school play, or you enjoy painting or sculpting. Perhaps you worked with the disabled or elderly as a volunteer. Any of these could help you in your job. You want to give potential employers as accurate a picture as possible of who you are and what you have to offer.

PUTTING IT ALL TOGETHER

- Be concise with your statements. Say what you need to in the least number of words. List your education and work experience in the order of most recent to oldest.

- Do not list your weaknesses.

- Ask your instructor or someone who is already employed in the field to read over your résumé, and listen to his or her advice.

- Try to keep your résumé to one page. Research has shown this length to be most effective.

- Use a word-processing program to create your résumé. A laser printer is the best printing method, but a good-quality inkjet printer will do. If you do not have access to a computer, use a typewriter or have your résumé professionally prepared.

- Even if you use a spell checker, be sure to read your finished résumé over several times for spelling and grammatical errors. Have a friend read it too.

DO I NEED A COVER LETTER?

The answer to this question is absolutely, Yes. A cover letter is a friendly way to introduce your résumé and let the reader know you are applying for an advertised job. All you need is four to five short paragraphs. If you have a computer, it is easy to compose one generic cover letter that you can then tailor to each potential employer by including the name and address of the salon, the name of the person who will review the résumé, if possible, and where you saw the ad or learned of the opening. A sample cover letter to accompany the résumé for our hairstylist is shown on the next page.

As you review this sample, note the important features of any cover letter that you would want to send a prospective employer along with a copy of your résumé.

1. It is friendly in tone and to the point.

2. It contains the name of the potential employer and the address of the establishment.

3. It indicates where you saw the ad or how you learned of the opening.

Holly Hairstylist
123 Meadowbrook Lane
Anytown, USA 12345

June 4, 2000

Ms. Joan Clipper
Oooh-La-La Salon
45 Main Street
Anytown, USA

Dear Ms. Clipper,

I am writing in response to your ad for a professional hairstylist that appeared in the *Anytown News* on Sunday, June 3. I graduated last month from Midwest Beauty College, and have just received my license in the mail.

I have enclosed my résumé, which details my previous work experience and education.

I am interested in joining a salon where I can make the most of my education and am also eager to continue to learn. I feel I am well qualified for this position and can make a significant contribution to Oooh-La-La Salon.

I would welcome the opportunity for a personal interview.

Sincerely,

Holly Hairstylist
Holly Hairstylist

In the next chapter, we'll cover where to look for jobs and how to interview effectively.

Holly Hairstylist
123 Meadowbrook Lane
Anytown, USA 12345
Phone: (555) 123-4567

JOB OBJECTIVE: Position as a professional hairstylist

**SUMMARY OF
QUALIFICATIONS:**   Solid training in the fundamentals of hair care and design, esthetics, and manicuring. Highly motivated and responsible with good time management skills; genuinely enjoy interacting with people of all ages and from all backgrounds.

EDUCATION: Midwest College of Beauty Culture, Pretty Place, USA
1999–2000
- Completed 1,400-hour cosmetology course
- 750 hours in school salon in hair, nail, and skin services
- superior scores on all written exams
- passed state licensing exam, June 2000

1998 Graduate, Anytown High School

WORK EXPERIENCE: Food Server, Fisherman's Cove, Anytown, USA
June–August 1997   *Duties:* Determined customer needs and filled them courteously; worked in a fast-paced summer tourism environment; cooperated with a team; learned to use a computer.

September 1997–   Retail Salesperson, The Gap, Oaks Mall
January 1999   *Duties:* Assisted customerswith selections; participated in sales training seminars; supervised two part-time employees; created attractive window displays.

REFERENCES: Mrs. Della Gregg, Instructor
Midwest School of Beauty Culture
1400 Main Street
Pretty Place, USA 56789
(555) 890-1122

Mr. John Hawthorne, Manager
The Gap, Oaks Mall
Anytown, USA 12345
(555) 890-1314

Additional References Available on Request

RESOURCES

Haft, Timothy D. *Trashproof Résumés*. New York: Random House, 1996.

Morin, Laura. *Every Woman's Essential Job Hunting and Résumé Book*. Holbrook, MA: Bob Adams, Inc., 1994.

A FEW KEY POINTS TO REMEMBER

- Make sure you follow all of the steps necessary to apply for and take the licensing exam.
- A résumé is like an advertisement for yourself.
- Many skills transfer from one job to another.
- Write a generic cover letter, and individually tailor it to accompany each résumé you send.

CHAPTER FIFTEEN

Finding Your First Job

Y ou've graduated from beauty school. You've passed the state boards with flying colors. You've prepared a dynamite résumé and a basic cover letter. Now it's time for some footwork.

WHERE TO FIND OPENINGS

JOB PLACEMENT CENTERS

Check first with your school's placement center. Salons seeking new employees routinely recruit directly from schools. This is especially true of chain salons, a popular place for new graduates to gain experience and build clientele while receiving the security of an hourly wage and health insurance. Sometimes the recruiting salons send representatives right to the school to give a group presentation of what they have to offer you. You may be able to fill out an application and have an on-the-spot interview.

NEWSPAPER ADS

Another source of job openings is the classified section of your local newspaper. The most ads appear on Sunday. Look for a heading like "Personal and Beauty" or "Beauty Professionals." The following advertisement ran in the Sunday, November 28, 1999 *Fort Myers News-Press*. The ad also included a phone number.

This ad gives you a good idea of what the employer can offer you, as well as what kind of people the salon is looking for to fill its job slots. (We'll get to that part a little later.) The same day, the paper included ads for nail techs and stylists at two resort/spas, an ad for a hair designer, nail tech, and receptionist (three separate positions) at a salon, and an ad announcing salon stations for rent for stylists and nail techs.

FIRST CHOICE Haircutters
Hairstylists WANTED

Our hairstylists are talented, vibrant, and energetic people who ensure the highest quality of customer service standards. Due to our fantastic growth and success, we are seeking dynamic people to join our new salons at South Pointe, Hancock Bridge, and Orange Grove area.

As Employer of Choice, we offer:
- Excellent Hourly Wage and Commission
- Excellent Bonus Program
- 401(K) and Competitive Benefits
- Paid Vacation and Holidays
- Professional Annual Training and Education
- Stability, Growth and Advancement
- Opportunities
- Great Work Environment

Come Join Our Winning Team.
HIRING AT ALL LOCATIONS

ANSWERING A CLASSIFIED AD

Most ads give a phone number to call. Some ask that you fax your résumé. Still others want you to apply in person. Mark the ads that interest you with a highlighter or red pen, then carefully check to see what action they want you to take. The instructions for replying to the ad are usually at the bottom of the ad. If you call, simply say, "Hello, my name is _____. I'm calling about the ad in Sunday's paper for a _____. Is that position still available?" If the answer is yes, your next question should be, "When can I come for an interview?" We'll cover interviewing skills a little later.

JOB FAIRS

Job fairs or career fairs have become popular lately. They are usually held in a large meeting hall. Employers rent booths where they interview job seekers and hand out information about the benefits of working for their companies, the positions they have open, and so forth. The job fairs are often sponsored by the labor department, a community business group, or even the local paper. They are usually advertised well in advance. Call before you go to ask if any salons or spas will be represented. If you live in a vacation area and would like to work at an upscale resort, you may find job fairs a good way to make contact with the personnel department. Pick up an application, chat briefly, and find out if the resort has a salon and/or spa and who is in charge of hiring for them. You can send the application to that person's attention when you get home.

THE INTERNET

Our attempts to search for employment in the cosmetology field on the Internet were both disappointing and enlightening. The AOL and Yahoo! job search sites are primarily aimed at degreed job seekers. When we searched the web for salon jobs, we found what seemed to be a terrific discovery: "the largest job search database for the salon and spa industry," at *http://www.just-4-me.com*. While the site offers the versatility of being able to search for a specific field in a specific city, state, and country, our search didn't turn up much: three esthetician positions were listed for California, one massage therapist position was listed for Connecticut, and four hair professionals positions were listed for Michigan. You can submit your résumé here on-line, though, and if you are interested in working in a different state or country, you might be pleasantly surprised.

Another source we found was the message center at *http://www.beautytech.com*. It yielded 25 positions on the day we checked it, and it offers the advantage of being able to network with other beauty professionals. One message there directed us to *http://www.bwdirectory.com*, the Beauty World Directory site. While not actually a job listings site, we did find nine jobs. One was in the United Kingdom, one in Spain, and one at a spa in British Columbia. It could be a valuable job search tool if you are seriously considering beginning a whole new life in another area!

One of the best Internet job sites for the cosmetology industry can be found at the NACCAS web site, *http://www.naccas.org*. On the day we checked it, there were 1,655 jobs advertised. You can post your résumé at this site, and search a directory of employment with chain salons. *SNIP* magazine (*http://www.snipmagazine.com*) yielded jobs at 18 salons around the country. Most were advertising for more than one position. *SNIP* is an entertaining and informative site, even if you don't find your dream job there. You'll enjoy reading articles on-line and looking at the latest award-winning hairstyles from all over the world.

KEEP YOUR EYES AND EARS OPEN

Another way to find job openings is to check visually for Help Wanted or Now Hiring signs as you pass by salons. If you're walking, stop in and ask. Even if that salon is not hiring, they may know of someone who is. By talking to people in the business, you can learn a lot of the inside information about working conditions at various salons that you will not learn anywhere else.

EFFECTIVE INTERVIEWING

Once you have located some job openings that interest you, follow the ad's directions for replying by calling and/or sending your résumé and a cover letter. In a few days, you will probably have some interviews lined up. You can use those few days to practice interviewing and doing some research.

Research? That's right. See if any of the salons where you will be interviewing have a web site. (Most of the chains do.) Find out as much as you can about the company. You want to seem interested and informed. You will seem that way if you can add something to the interview like, "I understand you've opened three more salons in this area just this year. The company is really growing!" Ask friends and neighbors and your school instructors about the other salons on your list. Try to have at least one "interested and informed" statement to make at each interview.

There is another reason for research. Good cosmetologists are in demand, and that makes the job market a very favorable one for you. While you might be tempted to jump at the first job offer, you should evaluate each potential employer as carefully as they will evaluate you. As a new graduate, you are looking for a place to gain experience, to learn more about your profession, and to develop new skills. Ask yourself if the employers you are considering will give you the opportunities that will help to advance you along your career path.

Another important factor for beginners is the opportunity to build a client base. Do the employers you are considering advertise to attract new clients, clients who could become your regular customers? Are the salons located in high-traffic areas where you will be able to depend on a certain amount of walk-in traffic?

Plan ahead what you will wear. One good interview outfit is all you'll need, because no one will see you more than once. Experts advise neutral colors and understated styles, so leave your platform sneakers in the closet. Since the job you seek is a creative one, you won't want to dress like a corporate executive, but try to wear something that is not especially noticeable except for its neatness. It should be comfortable to wear, too. Don't choose something that needs constant adjustment. Of course, you will want your hair, nails, and makeup to be impeccable. This may very well be more important for a cosmetology interview than in any other field!

Think about what salon owners are looking for, and how you can answer that need. The chart below will help you make the connections.

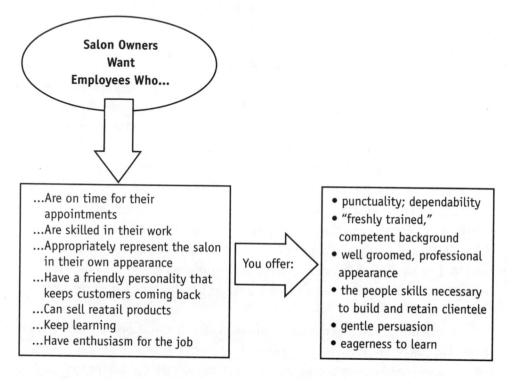

Salon Owners
Want
Employees Who...

...Are on time for their appointments
...Are skilled in their work
...Appropriately represent the salon in their own appearance
...Have a friendly personality that keeps customers coming back
...Can sell reatail products
...Keep learning
...Have enthusiasm for the job

You offer:

- punctuality; dependability
- "freshly trained," competent background
- well groomed, professional appearance
- the people skills necessary to build and retain clientele
- gentle persuasion
- eagerness to learn

Here are some additional tips for effective interviewing:

- Watch your body language. Don't slouch or twist up like a pretzel. Lean forward slightly to show your interest and openness, and make eye contact with the interviewer.

- Never gossip. Remember your mother's advice: If you can't say something nice about someone, don't say anything at all.

- While you are waiting to be interviewed, take advantage of the opportunity to eavesdrop. Most workplaces give off an aura of how the employees feel and of the general work atmosphere. Be wary if you pick up a lot of negative signals.

REHEARSING FOR THE INTERVIEW

Have a friend ask you the following questions as if he or she were the interviewer. These nine questions come up time and again at job interviews. As you compose answers, think about the key points you want to make about what you can offer the employer.

1. Tell me a little about yourself.

   Here you can mention that you've just become licensed and are very anxious to start using your skills. Show your enthusiasm for the beauty business.

2. What are your major strengths?

   You know what they are. Since the interviewer asked, don't be modest.

3. What are your weaknesses?

   Everyone has them. Find something that isn't really much of a weakness, for instance, "Sometimes I push myself too hard."

4. What sort of pay do you expect to receive?

   This is a good time to ask what sort of arrangements the salon is prepared to offer—straight commission, salary plus commission, or chair rental. As a beginner, you will probably be looking for a salary-plus-commission arrangement, but if steady money is not a concern, you might consider either of the other two. Just remember that with a chair rental arrangement, you will actually be putting money out—at first, maybe more than you bring in.

5. How does your previous experience relate to this job?

   Emphasize what you *liked* about other jobs you had, even if they were not in the beauty field. For instance, "I learned how to use a computer at the video store, and that was good. I always enjoy learning new things." Or, "Helping customers choose accessories to go with their clothing purchases was a lot of fun." Employers like people who are cooperative and get along with other employees, too. You might say, "Flipping burgers wasn't all that great, but the people I worked with were terrific and I enjoyed being part of the team."

6. Where do you see yourself going in the future?

   Just be honest. If you see yourself owning a salon some day, say so, but be careful not to give the idea that you plan only a quick stop-over here as an employee.

7. What will your former employers and/or instructors say about you?

   There is only one correct answer here. They will say you are competent, dependable, a hard worker.

8. Why do you want to work here?

   Here is where your research comes in. Say something good about the salon or the company. Say that you've heard good things about this workplace, that you would like to be part of the team.

9. Do you have any questions?

   You owe it to yourself to ask how many hours you would be expected to work, and what the hours would be. You may also want to find out if you have to provide your own supplies or if the salon provides them for everyone. Another concern is benefits. Does the company pay the premiums, or can you buy into a plan yourself?

There are only three steps left:

- Take a deep breath

- Believe in yourself

- Go for it!

RESOURCES

Fry, Ronald. *101 Great Answers to the Toughest Interview Questions.* 4th ed. Franklin Lakes, NJ: Career Press, 2000.

Krannich, Caryl Rae. *Interview for Success: A Practical Guide to Increasing Job Interviews, Offers, and Salaries.* Manassas Park, VA: Impact Publications, 1997.

A FEW KEY POINTS TO REMEMBER

- Some sources for job openings are school job placement centers, newspaper ads, job fairs, the Internet, and in-person inquiries.
- Research the salons where you will interview ahead of time to get some background information.
- Stage a few mock interviews with a friend.
- Dress appropriately for interviews and pay special attention to your hair, makeup, and nails.
- Be prepared to demonstrate your skills with a sample cut, facial, nail service—or all three.

Appendices

APPENDIX A—BOARDS OF COSMETOLOGY

Information changes frequently, so be sure to contact the agency listed for your state or province to get the latest update on requirements.

UNITED STATES

Alabama
Alabama Board of Cosmetology
100 N. Union Street, #320
Montgomery, AL 36130
Phone: (334) 242-1918
Fax: (334) 242-1926

Alaska
Alaska Division of Occupational Licensing
Board of Barber and Hairdressers
P.O. Box 110806
Juneau, AK 99811-0806
Phone: (907) 465-2547
Fax: (907) 465-2974

Arizona
Arizona State Board of Cosmetology
1721 F. Broadway Road
Tempe, AZ 85282-1611
Phone: (602) 784-4539
Fax: (602) 255-3680

Arkansas
Arkansas State Board of Cosmetology
101 F. Capital, Suite 108
Little Rock, AR 72201
Phone: (501) 682-2168
Fax: (501) 682-5640

California
California Barbering and
Cosmetology Program
P.O. Box 944226
Sacramento, CA 94244-2260
Phone: (916) 445-0713;
(800) 952-5210 (within CA only)
Fax: (916) 445-8893

Colorado
Colorado State Board of Barbers
and Cosmetologists
1560 Broadway, #1340
Denver, CO 80202
Phone: (303) 341-1454

Connecticut
Connecticut Department of Public Health
Cosmetology and Licensing
410 Capitol Avenue, MS #12 APP
P.O. Box 340308
Hartford, CT 06134
Phone: (860) 509-7569; (860) 509-8457

District of Columbia
District of Columbia
Department of Consumer and
Regulatory Affairs
Board of Barbering and Cosmetology
614 H Street N.W., Room 904
Washington, D.C. 20001
Phone: (202) 727-7474
Fax: (202) 727-7662

Delaware
Delaware Board of Cosmetology
and Barbering
Canon Building, #203
P.O. Box 1401
Dover, DE 19903
Phone: (302) 739-4522; (800) 273-9500
Fax: (302) 739-2711

Florida
Florida Department of Business
and Professional Regulation
1940 N. Monroe Street
Tallahassee, FL 32399
Phone: (850) 488-5702
Fax: (850) 922-6959

Georgia
Georgia State Board of Cosmetology
166 Pryor Street S.W.
Atlanta, GA 30303
Phone: (404) 656-3907
Fax: (404) 651-9532

Hawaii
Hawaii Department of Commerce
and Consumer Affairs
Board of Cosmetology
1010 Richards Street
P.O. Box 3469
Honolulu, HI 96801
Phone: (808) 586-3000; (808) 586-2699

Idaho
Idaho State Board of Cosmetology
1109 Main Street, #220
Boise, ID 83702-5642
Phone: (208) 334-3233
Fax: (208) 334-3945

Illinois
Illinois Department of
Professional Regulation
320 W. Washington Street, 3rd Floor
Springfield, IL 62786
Phone: (217) 782-8556
Fax: (217) 782-7645

Indiana
Indiana Professional Licensing Agency
State Board of Cosmetology Examiners
302 W. Washington Street, Room EO-34
Indianapolis, IN 46204
Phone: (317) 232-2980
Fax: (317) 232-2312

Iowa
Iowa Department of Public Health
Board of Cosmetology Arts and Sciences
321 F. 12th Street, 4th Floor
Des Moines, IA 50319-0075
Phone: (515) 281-4416
Fax: (515) 281-3121

Kansas
Kansas State Board of Cosmetology
603 Southwest Topeka Boulevard
(Suite 100)
Topeka, KS 66603-323
Phone: (785) 296-3155

Kentucky
Kentucky State Board of Hairdressers
and Cosmetologists
111 Street James Court
Frankfort, KY 40601
Phone: (502) 564-4262
Fax: (502) 564-0481

Louisiana
Louisiana State Board of Cosmetology
11622 Sunbelt Court
Baton Rouge, LA 70809
Phone: (504) 756-3404
Fax: (504) 756-3410

Maryland
Maryland Board of Cosmetology
500 N. Calvert Street, 3rd Floor
Baltimore, MD 21202
Phone: (410) 333-6320
Fax: (410) 333-6314

Massachusetts
Massachusetts Board of Cosmetology
100 Cambridge Street, Room 1406
Boston, MA 02202
Phone: (617) 727-9940
Fax: (617) 737-1627

Michigan
Michigan Department of Consumer and
Industry Services
Attn.: Cosmetology
P.O. Box 30018
Lansing, MI 48909
Phone: (517) 241-9201
Fax: (517) 241-9280

Minnesota
Minnesota Department of Commerce,
Cosmetology Unit
133 East Seventh Street
St. Paul, MN 55101
Phone: (651) 296-6319; (800) 657-3978
Fax: (612) 296-2886

Mississippi
Mississippi State Board of Cosmetology
P.O. Box 55689
Jackson, MS 39296-5689
Phone: (601) 987-6837
Fax: (601) 687-6840

Missouri
Missouri State Board of Cosmetology
P.O. Box 1062
Jefferson City, MO 65102
Phone: (573) 751-1052
Fax: (573) 751-8167

Montana
Montana Department of Commerce
Board of Cosmetology
111 N. Jackson
P.O. Box 200513
Helena, MT 59620-0513
Phone: (406) 444-4288
Fax: (406) 444-1667

Nebraska
Nebraska Department of Health
and Human Services
Regulation and Licensure
Credentialing Division
P.O. Box 94986
Lincoln, NE 68509-5007
Phone: (402) 471-2117; (402) 471-3577

Nevada
Nevada State Board of Cosmetology
1785 East Sahara Avenue, #255
Las Vegas, NV 89104
Phone: (702) 486-6542
Fax: (702) 369-8064

New Hampshire
New Hampshire State Board of
Barbering, Cosmetology, and Esthetics
2 Industrial Park Drive
Concord, NH 03301
Phone: (603) 271-3608
Fax: (603) 271-6702

New Jersey
New Jersey Board of Cosmetology
and Hairstyling
P.O. Box 45003
Newark, NJ 07101
Phone: (973) 504-6400
Fax: (973) 504-6400

New Mexico
New Mexico Board of Barbers
and Cosmetologists
P.O. Box 25101
Santa Fe, NM 87504
Phone: (505) 476-7110
Fax: (505) 827-7560

New York
New York Department of State
Division of Licensing Services
84 Holland Avenue
Albany, NY 12208-3490
Phone: (518) 474-4429
Fax: (518) 473-6648

North Carolina
North Carolina Board of Cosmetology
1201 Front Street, #110
Raleigh, NC 27609-7533
Phone: (919) 733-4117
Fax: (919) 733-4127

North Dakota
North Dakota Board of Cosmetology
1102 S. Washington Street
Bismarck, ND 58504
Phone: (701) 224-9800
Fax: (701) 222-8756

Ohio
Ohio State Board of Cosmetology
101 Southland Mall
Columbus, OH 43207-4041
Phone: (614) 466-3834
Fax: (614) 644-6880

Oklahoma
Oklahoma State Board of Cosmetology
2200 Classen Boulevard, #1530
Oklahoma City, OK 73106
Phone: (405) 521-2441
Fax: (405) 528-8310

Oregon
Oregon Board of Barbers
and Hairdressers
Licensing Programs
700 Summer Street N.E., #320
Salem, OR 97310
Phone: (503) 378-8667
Fax: (503) 585-9114

Pennsylvania
Pennsylvania Cosmetology Board
P.O. Box 2649
Harrisburg, PA 17105
Phone: (717) 783-7130

Rhode Island
Rhode Island Department of Health
Division of Hairdressing and Barbering,
Room 104
3 Capitol Hill
Providence, RI 02908-5097
Phone: (401) 222-2511; (401) 277-2827
Fax: (401) 222-1272

South Carolina
South Carolina Board of Cosmetology
P.O. Box 11329
Columbia, SC 29211
Phone: (803) 896-4494
Fax: (803) 896-4484

South Dakota

South Dakota Cosmetology Commission
500 E. Capitol
Pierre, SD 57501
Phone: (605) 773-6193
Fax: (605) 224-5072

Tennessee

Tennessee Board of Cosmetology
500 James Robertson Parkway
Nashville, TN 37243-1147
Phone: (615) 741-2515
Fax: (615) 741-1310

Texas

Texas Cosmetology Commission
P.O. Box 26700
Austin, TX 78755-0700
Phone: (512) 454-4674
Fax: (512) 454-0399

Utah

Utah Division of Occupational and
Professional Licensing Board of
Cosmetology
160 East, 300 South
P.O. Box 45805
Salt Lake City, UT 84145-0805
Phone: (801) 530-6628
Fax: (801) 530-6511

Vermont

Vermont Office of Professional
Regulation
Attn.: Cosmetology
109 State Street
Montpelier, VT 05609-1106
Phone: (802) 828-2373
Fax: (802) 828-2384

Virginia

Virginia Department of Professional
Occupation and Regulation
Board of Cosmetology
3600 W. Broad Street
Richmond, VA 23230
Phone: (804) 367-8509
Fax: (804) 367-2475

Washington

Washington Department of Licensing
Cosmetologist Licensing Program
P.O. Box 9045
Olympia, WA 98507-9045
Phone: (360) 753-3834
Fax: (360) 664-2550

West Virginia

West Virginia Board of Barbers
and Cosmetologists
1716 Pennsylvania Avenue, #7
Charleston, WV 25302
Phone: (304) 558-3450
Fax: (304) 558-3450

Wisconsin
Wisconsin Department of Regulations
and Licensing
Barbering and Cosmetology
Examining Board
P.O. Box 8935
Madison, WI 53708-8935
Phone: (608) 266-5511;
　　　(608) 266-2112
Fax: (608) 267-3816

Wyoming
Wyoming Board of Cosmetology
2515 Warren Avenue, Suite 302
Cheyenne, WI 82002
Phone: (307) 777-3534
Fax: (307) 777-5700

CANADA

Alberta
Department of Advanced Education and
Career Development/Apprenticeship and
Industry Training
10th Floor, City Centre
10155-102 Street
Edmonton, AB T5J 4L5
Phone: (403) 427-4601
Fax: (403) 422-5125

British Columbia
Board of Examiners. Hairdressers
Association of British Columbia
899 W 8th Avenue
Vancouver, BC V5Z IE3
Phone: (604) 871-0222
Fax: (604) 871-0299
E-mail address: *info@habc.bc.ca*

Manitoba
Department of Education and Training
1010 401 York Avenue
Winnipeg, MB R3C OP8
Phone: (204) 945-0910
Fax: (204) 948-2346

New Brunswick
New Brunswick Hairdressers Association
299 York
Fredericton, NB E3B 3P2
Phone: (506) 458-8087
Toll free: (800) 561-8087
Fax: (506) 458-1354

Newfoundland
Department of Education,
Industrial Training Division
P.O. Box 8700
St. John's, NF AlB 4J6
Phone: (709) 729-2729
Fax: (709) 729-5878

Northwest Territories
Department of Education, Culture and
Employment
Box 1320
Yellowknife, NWT X1A 2L9
Phone: (403) 920-3422
Fax: (403) 873-0200

Nova Scotia
Cosmetology Association of Nova Scotia
75 MacDonald Avenue #9
Dartmouth, NS B3B IS5
Phone: (902) 468-6477
Fax: (902) 468-7147

Ontario
Ministry of Education and
Training/Apprenticeship Services
1-625 Church Steet
Toronto, ON M7A 2B5
Phone: (416) 326-5800
Fax: (416) 326-5799

Prince Edward Island
PEl Hairdressers Association
P.O. Box 984
Charlottetown, PC C1A 7M4
Phone: (902) 892-5359

Saskatchewan
Department of
Education/Apprenticeship Division
3085 Albert Street, Room 226
Regina, SK S4P 3V7 Canada
Phone: (306) 787-2444
Fax: (306) 787-5105

Yukon
Government of Yukon, Corporate Affairs
Box 2703
Whitehorse, YK YIA 2C6
Phone: (867) 667-5811
Fax: (867) 667-6339

APPENDIX B—RESOURCES

SPECIFIC CAREERS

Ashley, Martin and Lorrie Klosterman. *Massage—A Career at Your Fingertips*. Carmel, NY: Enterprise Publishing, 1999.

Church, Susan. *Permanent Cosmetics A to Z*. Newport Beach, CA: Action Publishing, 1998.

Gambino, Henry J. *The Esthetician's Guide to Business Management*. Albany, NY: Milady Publishing Corp., 1994.

Miller, Erica T. *Salonovations' Day Spa Techniques*. Albany, NY: Milady Publishing Corp., 1996.

Wright, Crystal A. *The Hair, Makeup and Styling Career Guide*. Los Angeles, CA: Set the Pace Publishing Group, 1997.

JOB SEARCH

Bolles, Richard Nelson and Dick Bolles. *What Color Is Your Parachute? 2000*. Berkely, CA: Ten Speed Press, 1999.

Grappo, Gary Joseph and Adele Lewis. *How to Write Better Résumés*. Hauppauge, NY: Barron's Educational Series, Inc., 1998.

Wilson, Robert F. *Conducting Better Job Interviews* (Barron's Business Success Series). Hauppauge, NY: Barron's Educational Series, Inc., 1997.

PROFESSIONAL DEVELOPMENT

Cotter, Louise and Frances London Dubose (contributor). *The Transition: How to Become a Salon Professional*. Albany, NY: Milady Publishing Corp., 1996.

D'Angelo, Allen. *Fun, Creative and Profitable Salon Marketing: 67 Ways to Grow Your Salon Business*. College Station, TX: Archer-Ellison Publishing, 1998.

Lamb, Catherine. *Milady's Life Management Skills for Cosmetology, Barber-Styling, and Nail Technology*. Albany, NY: Milady Publishing Corp., 1996.

Hoffman, Lee. *Salon Dialogue: For Successful Results*. Albany, NY: Milady Publishing Corp., 1998.

Lewis, Jerre G. and Leslie D. Renn. *How to Start and Manage a Hair Styling Salon Business: Step by Step Guide to Managing Your Own Business*. Lewis and Renn Associates, 1999.

Misner, Ivan. *The World's Best-Known Marketing Secret: Building Your Business With Word-of-Mouth Advertising*. Austin, TX: Bard Press, 1999.

Oppenheim, Robert. *101 Salon Promotions*. Albany, NY: Delmar, 1999.

Spear, Elaine J. *Salon Client Care: How to Maximize Your Potential for Success*. Albany, NY: Milady Publishing Corp., 1999.

WEB SITES

ACE Grants:
http://www.ace-grant.org

Aesthetics International Association:
http://www.beautyworks.com/aia

American Massage Therapy Association:
http://www.amtamassage.org

American Salon:
http://hairnet.com

Beauty Professionals Network:
http://www.beautytech.com

Salonweb:
http://www.salonweb.com

Society of Permanent Cosmetic Professionals:
http://www.spcp.org

MAGAZINES

American Salon
270 Madison Avenue
New York, NY 10016

Dermascope
3939 East Highway 80, Suite 408
Mesquite, TX 75150

1st Hold
4237 Los Nietos Drive
Los Angeles, CA 90027-2911

Les Nouvelles Esthetiques
306 Alcazar Avenue, Suite 204
Coral Gables, FL 33134

Modern Salon
P.O. Box 1414
Lincolnshire, IL 60069

Nailpro
7628 Densmore Avenue
Van Nuys, CA 91406-2042

Nails
21061 S. Western Avenue
Torrance, CA 90501

Salon News
P.O. Box 5035
Bentwood, TN 37024-9809

SalonOvations
3 Columbia Circle
Albany, NY 12212-2519

Skin, Inc.
362 South Schmale Road
Carol Stream, IL 60188-2787

PROFESSIONAL ASSOCIATIONS AND TRADE ORGANIZATIONS

(Also see "Web sites.")

American Association of Cosmetology
Schools
15825 North 71st Street, Suite 100
Scottsdale, AZ 85254
Phone: (800) 831-1086
Web site: *http://www.beautyschools.org*

American Beauty Association
401 North Michigan Avenue
Chicago, IL 60611
Phone: (800) 868-4265
Web site: *http://www.americanbeauty.org*

Associated Bodywork and Massage
Professionals
28677 Buffalo Park Road
Evergreen, CO 80439-7347
Phone: (800) 458-2267
Web site: *http://www.abmp.com*

American Electrology Association
106 Oak Ridge Road
Trumbull, CT 06611
Phone: (203) 274-6667
Web site: *http://www.electrology.com*

Beauty and Barber Supply Institute,
Inc.
11811 N. Tatum Boulevard #1085
Phoenix, AZ 85028-1625
Phone: (800) 468-2274
Web site: *http://www.bbsi.org*

Cosmetology Advancement Foundation
208 East 51st Street
New York, NY 10022
Phone: (212) 388-2771

The Day Spa Association
P.O. Box 5232
West New York, NJ 07093
Phone: (201) 865-2065

International Guild of Professional
Electrologists
803 North Main Street
High Point, NC 27262
Phone: (800) 830-3247
Web site: *http://www.igpe.org*

National Accrediting Commission of
Cosmetology Arts and Sciences
901 North Stuart Street
Arlington, VA 22203-1816
Phone: (703) 527-7600
Web site: *http://www.naccas.org*

National Association of Barber Boards
77 South High Street, 16th floor
Columbus, OH 43266-0304
Phone: (614) 466-5003

National Cosmetology Association
401 N. Michigan Avenue
Chicago, IL 60611
Phone: (312) 644-6610
Web site: *http://NCA-now.com*

The Salon Association
11811 N. Tatum Boulevard, Suite 1085
Phoenix, AZ 85028-1618
Phone: (800) 211-4TSA
Web site: *http://www.salons.org*

Index